MW01171130

C. J. Loray Media Group
Clarice L. Johnson
Senior Editor/Publisher
Sterling Heights, Michigan
586.843.4161

Cover Design
The HMG Agency
L'Oreal Hartwell
Saginaw, Michigan
810.210.2336

Copyright © 2019 by Christopher Mike
All rights reserved. No part of this book may
be reproduced, scanned, or distributed in any
printed or electronic form without expressed
permission.
First Edition: October 2019
Printed in the United States of America

ISBN – 9781701635784

*Some names and identifying details have been changed to
protect the privacy of
individuals.*

All scripture taken from KJV unless specified otherwise.

FROM

HUMILITY

TO

HONOR

CHRISTOPHER MIKE

DEDICATION

To my wife, Anika and my children Andrea (Renee) Coleman, Christopher, Kala, Akina, and Kearsen Mike

To all my pastors: Rev Thurmond Tillman, Bishop Alvernis Johnson, Bishop Jerry Hutchins, and the late Donald Curlin

With much gratitude and appreciation to Dr. Gertrude Stacks and my Chief Apostle Garfield Curlin

It is my prayer that you see that my life is a testimony of your labor and prayers. Thank you all for believing in me. I am grateful for your love and guidance; without you in my life this book would have never been written.

Special Tributes

The Late Mr. And Mrs. Edward (Helen) Mike

I will like to say thank you for all that you have done in my life. You could have chosen to be the worst parents in the world instead you were the best. You were the best providers a child could ever hope for. Your values were outstanding, and you taught me well. I love you both for being such great examples; miss you greatly.

The Late Mrs. Sarah Love

This woman of God was a strong matriarch who bared the very essence of her last name (Love). Mrs. Love was the grandmother that everyone hoped for. She was the cookies and milk type of granny; she never was too busy for anyone. She made many sacrifices and was committed to the call of being an example of our Lord and personal Savior. And the only time I could remember her raising her voice was when I got on her last nerves and she would say in a stern voice, "Luster Love pays the bills here!" Luster Love was her husband. Thank you, Mrs. Love, for taking the time to teach me about Jesus!

As long as the earth endures, seedtime and harvest will come.

The Late Dr. Estella Boyd

To my spiritual Mother, Dr. Estella Boyd: for it is now harvest time. Your labor of love was not in vain. I intend to make good on your prayers and sacrifice. You are greatly missed and appreciated. Thank you for believing in me and seeing beyond my doubts and fears.

Table of Contents

FOREWORD: Elect Lady Anika Mike

INTRODUCTION

PART I: THE LIFE, THE PROCESS, AND THE CALL

Chapter 1:   Humble Beginnings.......................15

Chapter 2:   Answering the Call.........................33

Chapter 3:   12 Years.............................…..…….42

Chapter 4:   The Preparation...........................58

PART II: WALKING OUT THE PROCESS INTO THE APOSTOLIC

Chapter 5:   The Way Up is Down.....................68

Chapter 6:   Seat of Honor...........…...............79

Chapter 7:   From Humility to Honor.................88

          Part I: What is Humility

          Part II: What is Honor

Chapter 8:   The Office of an Apostle....................99

The Final Words..106

Personal Messages from the Writing Team:

- Joyce, C.
- Odom, E.
- Okwu, A.
- Pritchard, J.
- Wynn, D.

Closing Remarks to Writing Team:

Pastor Christopher Mike

Appendix...117

Works Cited...133

FOREWORD

Blessings to you, my name is *Anika Mike*. I have had the awesome pleasure of being married to Christopher Mike for the past 29 years. Together we have five wonderful children: Andrea (Renae) Coleman, Christopher, Kala, Akina, and Kearsen Mike and 4 grandchildren Londyn, Skylar, Leilani, and Alieya.

I remember like it was yesterday the night Christopher called me excited because he had gone to a retreat and rededicated his life to the Lord. I remember him crying and saying that the Lord has called him to minister. From that day until now I have seen tremendous growth and change. The Lord has moved miraculously through Christopher, using him to heal, deliver, and bless the people of God.

This book is a true testimony of some of the things that he endured on his journey to being able to walk in the true anointing that God has placed him in. He opens up about some of the trials he faced and how he passed or failed the trial, along with the outcomes.

By reading and finding yourself in the book it can help you navigate successfully through your own journey, understanding where you are and how to not abort the process. Recognizing that joy and happiness can be yours if you go through the process and that greater is on the other side of your wilderness.

Elect Lady Anika Mike

To My Husband

I just want you to know how proud of you I am, first for fighting and standing through the storms, for never giving up when it seemed as though the world was against you. Mostly for allowing the Lord to have his way in your life. All of that has made you a husband that can pray death off me, one that can lead, hold and comfort me through anything. A father that can see ahead and protect our children and now that they are adults they can run to for guidance and help. A grandfather that your grands are happy to call Papa. Truly today I am a blessed woman and I am looking forward to seeing what all God does for you, us in this next chapter of our lives. Love you, Anika

INTRODUCTION

The purpose of this book is to reveal the true heart of God concerning the Spirit of Humility and Honor. It's to fight one of the oldest sins since the beginning of time: PRIDE. Pride is the spirit that caused Satan to be cast out of heaven and the very same spirit that has compelled many today, to be resisted by God. Satan fell because of pride that originated from his desire to be God instead of a servant of God. This book will help you to identify, in your own life, the things that are stopping you from elevating and reaching your God given purpose. I will expound on my experiences that adversely impacted my life. I will expose the profound challenges that were scattered amongst the heartbreak that proverbially attempted to snatch my predestined place of honor in God. I will openly share the deep revelations that I received by the Holy Spirit which will, hopefully, open your eyes to the spirit of pride. Ultimately, the words that flow

> Pride is the spirit that caused Satan to be cast out of heaven and the very same spirit that has compelled many today, to be resisted by God.

out of my spirit in this literary journey, will expose the enemies' wicked desires to steal, kill, and destroy your destiny. By the time you have completed these eight chapters, you will be equipped and well informed to receive everything you need to finish this race with success and power.

Apostle Christopher Mike

PART I:

THE LIFE,
THE PROCESS,
AND THE CALL

Chapter 1
Humble Beginnings

Since the beginning of my life, struggle had been a mainstay, and Satan even tried to block my entrance into the world. The doctors told my mother that she could not have any more children, after having a pregnancy that ended in a miscarriage, which almost took her life. Months later; my mother found out that she was pregnant with me. The physicians told her the only option was to abort me because there would be a "fifty-fifty" chance that she or I could die.

The day I came into the world was a clear October day, not a cloud in the sky. It was an unseasonably balmy seventy degrees and the leaves were beginning their transition from a luscious green, to the magical fall colors of red, orange and yellow. My arrival came during the mid-morning shift change, at 9:35 am to be exact. I was born two months early, weighing three pounds and seven ounces. The interesting thing was, my birth certificate wasn't secured until the next day because they didn't expect me to live. So, I was really born on October 18, 1967, but I celebrate my birthday on October 19th. Well actually, I celebrate both days. Why not? I stayed in the hospital three extra months and my parents took me home in an incubator, that had to be at a certain temperature, at all times. Even though the devil tried to take my life, little did he know, God had a plan and he could not stop that plan!!!

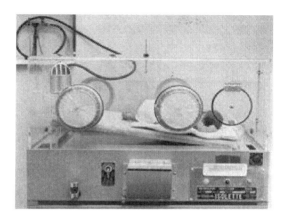

In those days, incubators were huge. Not like the size they are today.

My family history was not your typical, traditional Christian background, although my parents loved God. They taught us to respect church. They taught us to respect pastors and to not play with God. We were raised in a household where if it were thundering and lightening, we were told to sit down because God was talking; we'd cut off the lights and not move until God was finished. We were taught to never question God about anything, because God was sovereign. He's always right and never wrong. Additionally, we were taught that there is a Heaven and there is a Hell. We were admonished to live a good life in order to go to Heaven.

> We were taught to never question God about anything, because God was sovereign. He's always right and never wrong.

Although we were taught these things, our lifestyles contradicted the values they instilled in us. My environment consisted of gamblers, hustlers and fast money and a myriad of women for the men.

My family would sit around and have card games once a week. For example, on a typical weekend, there would be lots of food to be sold, such as sausage dogs, hot dogs, deviled crabs, chicken plates, with red rice or something of that nature. If your family hosted the weekly game, certain people would be invited to the festivities at your house to play cards: *Pity Pat or Deuces*. All the adults would have their beer and liquor. Whoever was hosting the card game, received a third of the pot, making it rather lucrative to be the host. Drinking, cussing, and fussing, in excess, was our typical weekend. I recall being about seven or eight years old at the table playing cards. I was good at it. I would win money every time I would play. I thought that was the way of life and felt like that was what I was supposed to do.

My parents worked long, arduous hours. My father was a longshoreman, while my mother was a factory worker. So, I was left at home a lot with my three older sisters. Therefore, I became a target for molestation. I learned to survive and protect myself, by any means necessary. We lived in a neighborhood where if anybody out there was a predator, I was a prey.

I remember the day when someone broke into our home and grabbed me. He pulled me into the basement and tried to molest me. I fought as hard as I could until I broke away. I ran and ran until I found some thick bushes to hide behind. As I looked through the dense leaves, I could see the legs of the person who was looking for me walk by. I was intently quiet and didn't move until that person went away.

I also remember being isolated a lot. The isolation I felt gripped my entire existence like a darkly colored room without any beams of light piercing the darkness. I was dreadfully alone. As I was repeatedly left alone, fear and rejection were evident in my life. I tried, to no avail, to express myself in ways I thought were good, but I was grossly misunderstood.

I was teased incessantly. I was called many bad names by my peers. I was called a fagot, a sissy, and a punk. I was also called weird. One day, while my friends and I were playing a game, they saw a name on the checkerboard. It said, "*Made by Whitman.*" They inadvertently mistook the name for "White Boy" and started calling me that as a cruel nickname. Then, instead of them calling me "White Boy," they would change the name and call me "Whitman." They would yell, "Get away from me, Whitman!" They taunted me for years, until I developed a dislike for the color of my skin and the way I looked. I had to deal with the stigma of being bullied. It was a rather trying and difficult time for me.

In my effort to escape, I gravitated towards the seemingly incomparable superhero movies in the world of make believe. They were strong, brave and able to beat up the bad guys. Superheroes were tall and grandiose. I was tiny in size and very small in stature. Any notorious superhero I thought was able to fight and win, I became them. Whether it was Wonder Woman, Superman, Batman, or Oh Mighty Isis. That was the only way I knew how to win against the bad guys that were trying to destroy me. These were some of the reasons why I had an imaginary friend. I named him Jesus, because He was my hero. He was someone that everybody looked up to, everyone respected. Even though, I didn't know much about Him, except for what mother my had taught me. I respected Him because He was a hero, and nobody messed with Jesus. And in that, I learned the power of the name, Jesus.

> Even though I didn't know much about Him. Except for what mother my had taught me. I respected Him because He was a hero, and nobody messed with Jesus. And in that, I learned the name Jesus.

Jesus, my imaginary friend, didn't have a face. He was more of a presence; more like an inward voice, who was totally separate from my emotions. No matter how afraid I was, when He said, "Be at Peace," I immediately got calm. That's when I knew He was real. He was always leading me, always talking to me. He was always a part of me.

So, I began talking to Him and would spend hours and hours with Him alone. We had this tree in our front yard that grew up against our home and covered the house. This looming and extraordinarily huge tree kept me from being seen outside while in the front yard. That is where I would go to talk to my imaginary friend, Jesus. I talked to Him when I got in trouble, when I was afraid, lonely, or felt rejected. Anytime anything negative happened, was when I went to talk to Him.

During this time, I met a boy named "Sweepy." I was around nine or ten years old. One day, while we both were riding our bikes, he invited me over to his house. Sweepy, a tall, chubby, bright eyed, rambunctious kid, whom everyone wanted to hang around, became the only friend I had for a while.

He took me down the street to his house and I met his grandmother, Mrs. Love. Her name described who she was, full of love, kindness and she cooked the best food I had ever tasted. She was the absolute epitome of what love really meant. I remember walking into her kitchen while she was cooking and smelling the greatest chicken and dumplings. I could never forget that day, because when she asked me if I wanted to eat dinner, I told her yes. Mrs. Love was the neighborhood grandmother everyone loved. Everybody in the neighborhood wanted to hang out at her house because that's where you got your fun snacks and delicious meals prepared in love.

We knew that when she went to the store, she shopped for the kids, as well. She had an open house policy…any child could come and grab some food and then go out and finish playing. To me, she was the perfect grandmother who also talked to me about God.

Sweepy and I became the best of friends and hung out every day. Although, every once in a while, Sweepy would get upset with me and we would go days without talking. The feelings of loneliness and rejection would resurface. However, I always had my imaginary friend, Jesus. I was so happy that He was still my friend. One time, my mom had given me an allowance and I buried it in the ground. I prayed over it and asked him to take it in exchange for being my friend. Then, I went off to school. I couldn't wait to get back home to see if He had taken it.

After getting off the school bus, I ran to the backyard and started to dig up the hole to see if the money was still there. Only to find that the money was still there. The feeling of rejection resurfaced once again, and I screamed from the top of my lungs, at my imaginary friend, "Forget you! Since, you don't want to be my friend, I don't want you to be my friend either. Forget you, you don't have to be my friend!" I took the money, ran to the store and bought a bunch of candy and went back home. I remember being so upset with Jesus that I said to myself, "I'm going to eat all of this candy and I don't have to have Him as a friend."

As I began to eat the candy, I dozed off to sleep. When I woke up, the cartoon *Tom and Jerry* was on the television. Tom, the cat, was chasing Jerry, the mouse, with a hammer. He then hit Jerry on the head. The knot came up out of Jerry's head and he fell backwards onto the ground. Then, I saw Jerry's spirit float up like a bright, hollow shadow and Jesus began to speak to me in a childlike manner. He said, "This is how I received your sacrifice." I witnessed Jerry's spirit float up and his body was still lying down. In my heart, I knew by that demonstration, that though my money may have been there physically, Jesus have received my sacrifice spiritually. He allowed me to see and experience the demonstration that I may get the spiritual understanding of it.

After having that vision, in much excitement, I went to visit Mrs. Love the next day and told her all about it. She was the one who sparked my interest in Jesus. That's when I made up in my mind to find out more about Him. Who is this Jesus

> Who is this Jesus that everyone talks about and respects?

that everyone talks about and respects? I started going to church. The church that I attended was Bethlehem Baptist Church. I went with a friend in the neighborhood. There, I began to learn more about who Jesus was. When I started finding out who He was, I promised myself, I would not gamble anymore. I decided, I was going to change my life from what I was experiencing as a young boy. I made up in my mind I wanted Jesus, making Him my personal Savior. My hunger for Jesus was so intense and I desired to be in His presence so much that I would have communion with Him. I would start by getting the bread, then I would pour the Kool-Aid, or whatever there was to drink at that time. I'd take a bath and drape myself in sheets and kneel before a candle to pray to Him. At a very young age, I began having visions and dreams. He would talk to me about my family and life. The more He would talk to me, the more questions I had, although, I had not been filled with the Holy Spirit, yet. Mrs. Love told me that being filled with the Holy Spirit would transform my life.

 One day I was over at Mrs. Love's house. She was telling me about the move of God that was taking place at her church. People from all over the place were being healed. She told me I had to come visit her church to see how the power of God was moving mightily. She asked me, "Do you want to come to my church next Sunday?" I said, "Yes!" I wanted to see the healing that Mrs. Love was talking about.

After we had finished talking, I left her house and ran home. As I was running home, I had my head down and ran into this tall man. He grabbed me by both of my shoulders and emphatically asked me, "Son, do you read your bible?" I screamed, "No Sir!" He then yelled, "Read your bible!" I jerked away from him in complete shock and fear. I took three steps, looked back and abruptly he was gone.

About a year later, I was at Mrs. Love's house again, talking about the Lord. As I left, still making that trek to try to make it home before the streetlights came on, I bumped into the same man again. He grabbed me and asked again, "Son, do you read your bible?" I answered, "No Sir." He sternly said, "I told you to read your bible!" I jerked away from him again, ran about three steps, looked back and he was gone again in a flash. That's when I concluded, "Lord, I just got to get a bible. I got to get this bible because this man keeps telling me to read the bible!" I asked myself, "Where in the world can I find a bible?"

Thankfully, I finally made it back home, scared and out of breath, I tried to figure out why had I run into the same tall, overarching man bellowing the same words. As I laid in the bed that evening pondering my scattered thoughts, I heard a voice say, "Go up in the attic. There's a Bible in there." I had never been up there. In fact, every time I passed by the attic, I would look up at it, contemplate opening the door, then swiftly ran by. I was certainly shaken, because I heard this voice tell me to go up in this dark, dark place! I was literally and utterly afraid of the dark. I was afraid to go into the attic because that brought back the fear and anxiety that came as the result of the close encounter with molestation in the basement. It had the same type of door and same type of stairs from my old house. Having tried to avoid every thought of being alone, I never wanted to be isolated or put back into that situation again. That fear followed me constantly. I would run past that attic every day going to my bedroom.

Now, I'm hearing a voice telling me to go in a dark, dusty, mite-filled attic to get a bible! Again, I heard the still calm voice tell me, "Go in the attic and look on the right-hand side in the corner." I finally built up enough courage to go into the attic and went to the back corner like the voice told me. I reached down and surely there  it was, a bible. It was a black, medium-sized bible that was old and dusty. My fearful heart leaped within me. I really heard God's voice!!! And…I OBEYED! *Side Note: When you hear His voice, obey! Do it the first time with joy and gladness!*

I then remembered that I was still in the attic. I turned around and bolted for the door, jumping down the stairs nearly falling and hitting the last step with my face. I busted through the door of my room, jumped into the bed and covered my head with the heavy blankets. Still clutching the old, dusty bible in my firm grip, I opened it and felt within myself that something was going to happen. As I closed my eyes, I opened the bible at the same time and immediately a feeling like that of which I have never felt before came over me. As I was reading the bible, the first words that came out of my mouth sounded like a foreign language I never spoke before. While speaking in this foreign language I immediately went to see Mrs. Love because I couldn't stop and she told me that was the Holy Spirit. I'll never forget that night.

As the years progressed, I began to go to First African Baptist Church, with my dad. My dad had made the decision to give his life to Christ. So, when he said he was going to be baptized my family came in from all over the United States. Everybody acted like it was a wedding; it was a major event and a big deal. I was so happy for my dad being baptized. I was like, "Wow, my dad is doing something huge and big." He got baptized, however, didn't attend one Sunday after that except for Easter, because that was the family church.

I had given my life to God already and really wanted to get involved in church. So, I got baptized, just like my dad. I wanted to emulate his decision to be close to God. But, being that we were just not churchy people, I never went back afterwards either. Like father, like son. It wasn't my intention to do that. I just didn't have the complete meaning, or true understanding of it all. It was difficult because of my surroundings. I was the only one in my family trying to give my life to God. I was the youngest and didn't have transportation to get to church. So, from about the ages of fourteen to eighteen years old, I didn't go to church at all.

I'll never forget my pastor who was new to the church. He was looking at all the members who weren't coming to church. He ran across my father's name, so he came and visited my dad. Then after seeing my name, he came back the next day and realized that we were father and son. He asked in bewilderment, "Why are y'all not coming to church?" I interjected, "Sir, I mean no disrespect, but I don't have to come to church." He continued talking to me and I thought I was big and bad, so I said, "Look man look, if God want me, I'll answer Him. I don't have to answer to you!" A few days later, he came back, and I went toe to toe with him again and screamed, "Like man, what do you want? Why are you bothering me?" He explained, "This is my last time coming to you, son!" He looked me in my face and said, "You will call me before I call you!" In that moment, I felt like, "Oh man! Heaven just fell on my head. Oh my God! I done messed up, God is mad with me. I done talked back to this man of God too much and now he cursed me. God gone get me!" From that moment, I was tormented. I remember being chastened by God in my dreams.

In Job 33:15-17, the bible says,

"In a dream, in a vision of the night,
when deep sleep falls on people
as they slumber in their beds,
16 he may speak in their ears
and terrify them with warnings,
17 to turn them from wrongdoing
and keep them from pride."

I didn't know the scriptures at that time, but I was living it. I remember having a dream one blistery cold night in December. In that dream, Jesus came to me. His countenance was low, as in that of disappointment. He didn't like the lifestyle I was living or the things I was doing. He was calling me to be used of Him. I'll never forget that it got to the place where I had no peace. I called my pastor and reminded him of our last conversation and pleaded for his help. He inquired about where I was, and I told him I was in Hilton Head at my sister's house. He asked me, "What's wrong?" I frantically asked, "Why won't He leave me alone. Why is God bothering me? Why I can't have no peace?" He tenderly explained to me, "God is calling you, son. If you get back here to Savannah, we're going to the Youth Convention at St. Simon's Island." He calmly said, "Don't worry about any money. Don't worry about anything. Just get to the church and on the bus."

I was about 18 years old then. That was, seemingly, the longest ride I had ever gone on. I felt so empty, so voided, so much fear, as if I had no purpose. I was just barely existing and tormented by the unnerving thought of death. It seemed like death lurked in every corner of my tired, aching mind. There was absolutely no peace, even in my sleep. It enveloped my very existence, like a piece of tattered mail, holding tightly to the ripped stamp of resistance plastered on my forehead. I felt like I was literally losing my mind. And my only hope was to answer God.

As we drove to the splendidly manicured St. Simon Island, I got off the old, stuffy bus feeling claustrophobic and dizzy from the rusted exhaust pipes under the beleaguered bus. There were all these young people my age, excitedly running around all over the place. Believe it or not, it was just so much distraction to me. I couldn't even get focused on why I came in the first place. Those pretty, young girls thought I was just this good-looking guy who was there to sweep them off their feet…the stuff that was going on at that campus was mind blowing.

I remember not being able to feel anything, as well as not having any peace at all. It became irritating. At this point, I just wanted to find out what God was saying. I wanted something from the Lord. I was trying to find myself and figure out why I had no peace. It was maybe five hundred or so churches there, at this huge youth convention. I went into the building feeling alone, confused and frustrated. I felt like this was finally it. I inwardly thought, "If I don't get God tonight, it's over." I humbly told the Lord, "Please, come into my heart. Come into my life and I am sorry for all my sins." I will never go back and do the things I did. I will not drink again. I will not get high again. I would really give my life to You, if You'd come into my heart." That night God led me outside and said, "I want to talk to you." I got up and walked out.

As I walked away from the noise of the convention center, suddenly, I turned to see the waves of the never ending, swaying ocean, with the brisk, winter breeze blowing on my face. I felt the fiery presence of God exploding through the waves and flowing across the waters headed straight for me. Please do not ask me how I knew it was God…I just knew! In an instant, He began to speak to me and said, "I called you to minister my word. You are mine and you belong to Me. I'm going to prove to you that I'm calling you." He continued, "Look around." I looked around and saw all those thousands of people there. He said, "Next year, I will make you the president over all of this."

I just broke into a deep, gut-wrenching cry. I was just so freshly saved and beginning to be renewed in the spirit of my mind. I asked Him, "Who are you going to make president over all of this? I don't know anything about church etiquette. I don't know anything about church, period. I don't know anything about the scriptures, preaching, teaching, or the word of God! I don't know anything about anything. I know absolutely nothing, and you mean to tell me you're about to make me the president over all of this?"

Still reeling from the extraordinary encounter, I just had with the Lord, and after I had gotten myself together, I went back inside and told my pastor what just happened on the waters. I explained to him, "God is calling me to preach!" He looked at me and asked, "Are you sure?" I said, "Yes!" He asked again, "Are you sure?" I said, "Yes, I'm sure." He said, "I want to ask you one question…can you live without doing it?" I said, "No!" He exclaimed, "Alright, praise God!"

My pastor had a smile that would make you feel like everything was going to be alright. He grabbed me and embraced me. I said, "That's not all God said. He said I was going to be the president over all of this next year." Well, one of the pastors overheard our conversation and yelled, "I'm sick of y'all lying on God. God ain't told you nothing!" I yelled back, "Yes, He did! He did tell me that!" He said, "God did not tell you that, son." I continued, "He did tell me that, man. Bro, look! I ain't got to tell you no more. I ain't even got to talk to you. I'm talking to my pastor." Then he said, "Well look! You tell God I said you ain't gone be the president over this, because I'm the one who chooses who will be the president over all this!" He said, "You will not be the president next year, so stop lying on God. I'm trying to help you." I told him, "Man, whatever!"

Well, the next year it was time for us to put in our ballots to run for president. I was sitting there saying, "God, I remember what you said. God, I don't like public speaking. I don't like to be in the forefront. I could barely read." He asked me, "What did I tell you to do?" So, I wrote my name down and put it in the basket. I filled out the application. That was the year that the President of the General Missionary Baptist Convention (GMBC) called the director and told him that this was the year that we were going to do something different. He was informed that he would not be allowed to select the president this year. Rather, the youth would choose who they wanted to be president.

My pastor turned around and looked at me square in the eyes and said, "I don't believe this is about to happen." My pastor was on the Board of Directors. He said, "God, I'm just watching!" So, while the committee was choosing the president, my name came up. They asked my pastor was I in good standing with his church and he said yes. He then said, "All the ballots and all the people's names were already pulled." Then, somebody stood up and asked, "What about that light-skinned preacher?" Everybody started screaming, "Yeah, we want him! We want him!" They raised their hands and voted. I became the president of the youth convention that night.

The thing about this is, my pastor came to the hotel room after midnight. He had on a trench coat and a hat, with it tilted downward. He looked up to me and said, "Be ready for tomorrow. That's all I got to say." Then he turned and left. The next day the official announcement came; I had been voted in as the President of the General Missionary Baptist Youth Convention for the State of Georgia. I really became the president, just like God said. That's when God started dealing with me tremendously at First African Baptist church.

Chapter 2
Answering the Call

My pastor came to me because I was moving in spiritual gifts to which the traditional Baptist church was not familiar. I was flowing heavily in the prophetic and having visions. God was healing people of sicknesses and diseases, giving me names of people and telling me that they were sick, and that He wanted to heal them. Although I never met them, my pastor knew the people. He would take me to their homes, as I would pray, they would get healed. This was happening so frequently that it was disrupting the traditional Baptist flow. I was really, truly different. However, they were not familiar with that kind of gift.

My pastor had called me to go with him to a ministers' retreat in Culloden, Georgia. It was nothing but preachers. I was the youngest one there. I remember having a dream while at the retreat. In this dream, an angel snatched me up and took me up into the heavenly places. He was going higher, higher and higher into the stratosphere. I saw things flicker past me at the speed of light. It was all happening so fast, I could hardly catch my breath. I asked the angel, "Am I dying? Is my life over?" That angel's eyes were so fixed, he never looked down at me. He held me tightly by the hand as we were flying towards this unknown destination. His gaze was fixed on his assignment and he was not bending. He just blatantly ignored me. I humbly posed a simple question to that angel, "Will I ever preach again?" He looked at me and prophetically pronounced, "You never were called to preach. You are a messenger!" Then, I woke up.

I was so distraught by the angel's sayings that I went and woke my pastor up out of his sleep. I told him, "I have to go and tell everybody God didn't call me to preach." As my pastor looked at me, I continued saying, "You mean to tell me God said He never called me to preach and that I'm just a messenger?" I kept bothering him, he got so aggravated and angry with me. He screamed, "Doggone Chris Mike! Go and study what a messenger is!" And when I did, I found out that a messenger means "Sent One." When you study out the apostles, you see that they are "The Sent Ones."

I recall having a dream about a young man who was a member of our church, that was involved in a shootout at Daffin Park. In the dream, I was standing in the middle of the park and could see the bullets whizzing pass me in slow motion. I could see bullets hit and miss some people. I remember looking into his face and calling his name. Then I woke up. I saw the majestic angels of the Lord lined up on both sides of me, as far as I could see. I looked up and there was a Divine Spirit in the middle. That spirit was like a beaming, bright light and the closer it got to me the smaller it became; like the size of a pill. It went down in my mouth. Then the Spirit spoke to me and said, "Fear not. It is I, said the Lord, never again question who you are in Me, for I have called you to be My Apostle."

> "Fear not. It is I, said the Lord, never again question who you are in Me for I have called you to be My Apostle."

Well at this time, I didn't even know apostles existed, other than the twelve apostles. Then the voice told me to intercede for those that I saw in the dream because Satan sought to take their souls that night. I immediately began interceding and praying. In my praying, I started to bind death. I rebuked anyone from being hurt. The next day it was on the news. There had been a shootout that involved the same people in the dream. Just like I saw it.

At work the next day, a friend came up to me and said, "Chris, may I see you in the back for a moment?" I said, "Yes." She said, "I want to give you something. The Lord woke me up about 3:00 AM this morning and told me to give it to you. It was a book titled "He Gave Gifts Unto Men," by Kenneth Hagin. When I got the book, I started devouring it and came across the three qualifications of an Apostle. One of those qualifications stated that one must have seen The Resurrection. So, I asked the Lord, "When have I seen you?" Immediately, the Lord took me back to the man that I met in the street and He said to me it was I, you met Me." When He told me that, the tears of gladness began to flow effortlessly from my eyes. That was the first time that I had gotten the understanding of who and what God was truly calling me to be.

God had begun using me mightily at First African Baptist Church. My pastor can attest to the fact that I would tell him things that were getting ready to take place in his church. He would come to me as if I were a secret counselor, like a person that he revered as a confidant to hear what God was saying concerning business meetings and situations at the church.

My pastor had a board meeting one day, and I remember someone standing up yelling at him saying, "We're not going to do what you're asking us to do!" They were fighting him on something that he wanted to do. The Holy Spirit stood me up and I told them, "God said, that you have disobeyed His manservant for too long and you are going to know that I have chosen this man by the sign of death." My pastor said, "Chris Mike, sit down!" So, I sat down. The next morning, he came to pick me up and he said, "I want to talk to you. You got a minute? Ride with me."

When we pulled up, it was the house of the person that stood up against him. The police were out there with the crime scene tape all around. I had asked my pastor what happened, and he said the person that you spoke to last night has fallen dead inside their home. Then, a week later at their funeral, their best friend had stood up and was giving remarks about how they were a great supporter. I leaned over and told my pastor that God said, "She's lying and she's going to die too." About two weeks later, she died. By that time, I had the pastor's undivided attention. There were different things God would tell me and I would tell him. God always did what He said He was going to do.

Jeremiah 1:5

"Before I formed you in the belly, I knew you; and before you came forth out of the womb, I sanctified you, and I ordained you a prophet to the nations."

I recall, one time the Lord woke me up talking to me and told me to run around my mother's house seven times. It was about 3:00 AM in the morning. I got up and started running around the house even times. As I was running around the third time, the Lord said, "A distraction is going to be there as you go around again but keep on running." By this time, it had started raining. My mom came outside and grabbed me and yelled, "You need to come in the house, son!" She exclaimed, "You done lost it!" She thought

I had lost my mind. I jerked away from her because God had told me to keep running. I kept running around the house and I was screaming at the top of my lungs, "Jesus! Jesus! Jesus!" I was running, like a mad man, around the house.
When I went back inside, my mom was sitting on the couch crying. She cried, "Baby come here. You have gone too far. You too deep. God don't do this kind of stuff to people." I assured her, "Mom you don't understand... He told me to run around the house seven times and rebuke death. All I know is to do what God told me to do!"

Immediately, someone knocked on the door extremely hard. Bam! Bam! Bam! Bam! Bam! Bam! Bam! My mother got up and ran to the door and exclaimed, "Who is it?" My brother said, "It's me, Momma! Open the door!" She opened the door and he fell in on the floor. He grunted, "Am I bleeding? Am I bleeding?" My mom searched his body for blood, and nervously asked, "Where? Where?" She frantically began checking him but didn't find any blood on him. He said, "Momma, I don't understand. I was hiding behind a bush and they shot up the bush." He screamed, "I don't know how a bullet didn't hit me!" She looked at me in amazement and bellowed, "Chris just told me that God told him to rebuke death and run around the house seven times!"

I recall my Momma hugging me and telling me. "I now understand what is happening with you, but you got something that is different." That night, my brother's life was spared, because I obeyed God.

You don't know what you're changing in the atmosphere when God tells you to do the seemingly bizarre things. Things that goes against the norm... You don't know why God is telling you to do these things, but He has a purpose and a reason.

"I'll take the foolish things of the world to confound the wise." 1 Corinthians 1:27

During services, God would use me so heavily in the Spirit. Sometimes, He would use me to pray for people who had cancer and different diseases and they would be healed by way of the laying on of hands and prayer. I would call strangers out by name and deal with their exact issues. Even in the midst of my pastor's sermons, he would give way for me to minister to people.

Until one day, my pastor came to me and said, "Your gift is different. People here aren't used to your gift." He informed me, "If God is calling you into the apostolic, you will have to be covered under an apostle who is somebody to teach you in the gift that you have. I can't do that." I got angry with him because I felt like he wanted to just get rid of me. He then told me that, "I'm not an apostle, but I will support you and will help you as much as I can." We started worshiping and having prayer meetings in my home. We would pray and people would be healed, delivered from demons and set free from addictions. I would teach the word and God would come in there mightily. We could sense the presence of God come in that place so powerfully, that it was blowing our minds. It consumed us. It grew so big to where people were all outside, down the street and cars were blocking other people's driveways. We had to find a place. But I would not say I would pastor, because I hadn't heard God say it.

> I believe that those who are truly chosen and hand-picked by God Himself has a time set when He calls you and you must answer. You really know his Voice the very first time He speaks. It's more of a will, a desire that is placed in your heart, than an audible voice spoken.

I believe that those who are truly chosen and hand-picked by God Himself has a time set when He calls you and you must answer. You really know His voice the very first time He speaks. It's more of a will, a desire that is placed in your heart, than an audible voice spoken. The Lord who formed us, knows for what particular services and purposes He intended for us.

I remember "The Call." I was fast asleep. And I had an out of body experience where I could literally see myself lying down next to my wife, Anika. I saw these great big hands and this ball of fire twirling. As the hands were twirling, the ball of fire kept getting bigger and bigger like an inferno. It appeared as though the hands threw the ball of fire at the house. I knew I had to get back into my body to save my wife and children. I jumped back into my body right before the fire hit.

Once it hit, it knocked my wife and I out of the bed. It flipped me over to the right side and my wife over to the left. She wasn't outside her body, and didn't see the vision, but she felt the effects of it. Then, the Lord spoke to me and said, "Feed my sheep. Feed my sheep!" I said, "Yes Lord! Yes Lord! Yes Lord!" While He's telling me this, she's saying, "Yes Lord," too. She doesn't hear what God is saying to me, but He's talking to her and she's saying, "Yes Lord!" That is when we started Resurrection Ministries of Christ. We moved from the house to the YMCA.

The Lord truly blessed the ministry. God moved mightily. However, meekness was something I lacked. The time came for my Assistant Pastor's appreciation. Our Hospitality Team had created for him a beautiful gift basket. However, I felt like the basket was rather small and insignificant. I also felt that the offering was too little. I felt like it wasn't enough money to give him. I remember standing up and grabbing the basket and calling the people cheap. I bellowed, "This is all you think of somebody who has labored for your life?" I took the basket and literally kicked it out of the church. The lady who had made the basket screamed and held her head down. I told her to hold her head up and she held her head up, with tears of humiliation and sadness just rolling down her eyes. When I started out with Resurrection Ministries of Christ the first time, I was arrogant. I was full of pride. I was mean and didn't take into consideration other people's feelings nor how the word left them feeling after I preached. I was dogmatic. I was a fire and brimstone pastor.

Chapter 3

12 Years

It wasn't until many years later, after I had shut down the ministry, that I realized how detrimental my actions were. For the sake of the people, it was crucial for me to have had a shepherd's heart. I had to learn the heart of God in order to become a shepherd that was after His own heart. I had to learn that God was a forgiving God, that God was a merciful God. He wasn't a God who was sitting on the throne ready to strike us down because of our errors and mistakes. I really felt that God at one point was so sick of me and my sins that I thought He was going to kill me. It wasn't until I spoke with a prophetess friend of mine. She told me that this was not the character of God. She said God loves you even in the midst of your sins.

> I had to learn the heart of God in order to become a shepherd that was after His own hear

In some churches, we teach either you get it right or you're going to hell. There's no in between. Sometimes, it's preached, if you don't want God, He doesn't want you either. That is not true. God wants us, even in the midst of our sins. He wants us to desire Him. He is love, joy, peace, long-suffering, kindness, goodness, faithfulness, gentleness, and self-control; the very essence of the fruit of the Spirit *Galatians 5:22-23*. Sometimes, we don't even realize these are the characteristics of who He is. We, as pastors, must be careful that we are not preaching a staunchly religious gospel but preaching in a kingdom perspective. It must not only be fire and brimstone, hell-bound preaching. That doesn't bring salvation to anyone. We must preach a balanced gospel. As preachers, we can't become "Judge and Jury" of the people. We must leave the people in God's hands and preach to bring salvation and deliverance and not to bring judgement, despair and fear. We must preach a gospel that states just as much as we sin, there is grace and mercy which is much more abundant towards us.

My church had gone from operating with over half a million dollars a year budget, to struggling to pay the mortgage and the bills at the church. I called a prophetess friend of mine and asked her could she help us out. She told me no. She informed me that it was time to close the doors of the ministry and enter a season of divine rest, healing, deliverance and restoration. At that time, I thought I was getting ready to travel and hit the nations. She admonished my wife and I to relocate to Saginaw, Michigan to come under my brother, for a season. It was time for my entire family to be restored. We relocated and lived in Michigan for five years and humbly received rest, restoration and rejuvenation to do the work of the Lord.

When we went to live in Saginaw, my wife and I had bought an all white house, in a prestigious neighborhood. It was a beautiful, three level home with five bedrooms. I thought I could still live the same lifestyle I was living. I lost a total four homes before realizing that God was trying to humble me. By now, our credit was so bad I thought I couldn't even get inside of an apartment. Then, God finally opened a door. Only God can have you leave a $300,000 home and come in and kiss the floor of a two-bedroom apartment with four kids, saying, "Thank You Jesus!"

When God has you in the course of humility, you can do everything imaginable to try to get out. However, you're going to stay there until you finish the course.

> **When God has you in the course of humility you can do everything imaginable to try to get out. However, you're going to stay there until you finish the course.**

Part of my course included watching my wife having to take a second seat, going from being a first lady to becoming a member of a church. If anyone knows a man, his pride and joy is his wife. It was challenging for me to see her humble herself in another woman's house. However, she did it with grace, and with honor. Although, I struggled.

I remember, my brother Bishop J and his congregation were trying to get into their new church. In an effort to get the building, the members were willing to sell their possessions and other significant things to assist the church with their building fundraiser. People gave cars, expensive China and furniture, jewelry and clothing. It was literally, mind-blowing!

During the fundraiser, I left to pick up Bishop J some dinner, and I said to the Lord, "Lord when you have me pastor again, I want you to give me members like this." The Lord yelled at me, and said, "How dare you!" When I heard His voice, I pulled the car over to the side and dropped my head in silence. He asked, "Do you remember the members that I gave you? They gave their life to the call that was on your life. Do you remember, Chris, they signed their names on the dotted line for you to get into the building you had? They gave what was more than silver and gold. They gave the integrity of their name; their credit. Do you remember how they sacrificed and worked tireless hours for your ministry?" I inwardly sunk with a slow reply, "Yes Lord. I remember." He interjected, "How dare you take it for granted." Again, I trembled, "Lord, I remember." He sternly replied, "Don't say anything! I want you to listen. Do you remember when you kicked the gift basket out the church?" I answered, "Yes Lord. I remember." He said, "I told you not to say a word." It was as if my heart stopped beating. The car became cold, and all I could hear was the silence of the air blowing on my shaken countenance. He continued, "Call her and apologize to her now."

I got on the phone and called her. She answered, "Hello." I said, "Hi, how are you? This is Pastor Mike." She said, "Hey Pastor Mike, how are you doing?" I answered, "I'm doing good. Do you remember years ago you made a beautiful gift basket for the assistant pastor's appreciation?" She replied, "Yes." I asked, "Do you remember what I did?" She answered, "Yes." I said, "I kicked the gift basket out of the church, and I called y'all cheap and stingy? I want to apologize, because God was not pleased. That was not the spirit of God and I am so, so, so, so sorry." She screamed on the phone and cried like somebody had died. With a sigh of relief, she responded, "You don't know what this has done for me today. For I had carried that moment all these years. I knew you were a man of God, but I couldn't hear you. I did that out of the kindness of my heart. I sacrificed and stayed up late to make it. But today, you calling to apologize and to say you're sorry, you don't know what that has done for me." She said, "I can hear you again." She has been one of my biggest supporters.

I went through those types of moments during my twelve-year sabbatical, where He was telling me about myself, who I was, what I did and how I disappointed Him. I didn't realize I still had pride and that I was allowing it to rule over me.

I want to make things crystal clear to you so that you may truly understand my process through this twelve-year sabbatical. It was a crucial time for my family and especially for me. There were times that our lives were in total shambles. It was horrible when it seemed like none of our prayers were being answered. However, it took me having to hit rock bottom to truly understand what was going on. Eventually, it took me losing everything I thought I wanted. God showed me how I had to confront my inability to identify who I really was in Him. He compelled me, through my adverse situations and circumstances, to learn *humility and honor.* Take my word for it…if you have a call upon your life, and God has set you on the path of righteousness, seek Him like never before. Allow the Spirit of God to enter your heart completely. Allow the Holy Spirit to be your guide, helper and paraclete.

God is Omnipresent…He's everywhere, at all times. God is Omniscient…He's all knowing.
God is Omnipotent…He is all powerful.

One of God's greatest Evangelists was hosting her conference at the Georgia Dome. She was doing a demonstration and asked a few of us to take part. As we were completing our assignment she yelled, "Hurry up! You're too slow!" in the microphone. When she said it, I knew that it was a rebuke. All I could think of was it being translated in many different languages, including sign language. I could hear the Spirit of God laughing at me. He asked rhetorically, "So, you still full of pride? Let me kill you!"

At the next conference she had, they had invited Anika and I to sit on stage with the other special guests. Now, I'm saying to myself, "Everybody sees me with one of the top evangelists of the world." I'm on stage with her, and my wife and I had been asked to be seated right behind her on the podium. I was sitting there full of pride in my Canali Suit, my alligator shoes and my Rolex watch. I thought I was dressed to "The T!" It felt good. I was like, "Yes Lord. God, you're really doing it!" Well, one of the workers came up and said, "Excuse me, Pastor Mike, Pastor 'So and So' just walked in. Do you all mind moving over just a little bit?" I said, "No, no problem." So, we moved over a little bit. We were still up there with a lot of dignitaries. She came back and said again, "Excuse me Pastor Mike, some other people just walked in. Do you mind sitting on the next row?" I answered, "That's good, no problem." So, they moved us back. After a while I said, "Anika, I know this girl ain't coming back up here again. Now this is ridiculous!" Sure enough, she came back and said, "There is a group that just came in. If you don't mind moving back two more rows." We moved so many times, until we were behind the curtains. Although we were behind the curtains, Anika just sat there looking gracefully still. She never paid me any attention with my attitude, as I became more and more perturbed. I was evidently crushed, but my pride was standing tall.

That's when the Lord called me out. He said. "Come outside with Me." I got up, walked behind the curtain and out of the arena. When I walked outside, it was drizzling. I recall the Lord saying, "Humble yourself!" I said, "Yes Lord." Again, He said, "I said, humble yourself!" The sound came down like a bolt of lightning and I fell to my knees in my Canali Suit and my alligator shoes. Then, He said, "I said, HUMBLE YOURSELF!" Although it was raining, without hesitation, I stretched out wide on the ground beside a trash can. He asked, "Do you want fame, or do you want me?" I humbly retorted, "God, I want you!" That's when He said, "Come on this journey with Me." Then, the Spirit lifted.

This was the same year Bishop J. was in the process of being elevated as a Bishop. He

> Do you want fame, or do you want me?

came to me and asked me to serve as his adjutant. I remember asking, "What is an adjutant? What would be my role as an adjutant?" This assignment was personal to me. I took it very seriously, so I researched to find out what an adjutant to the Bishop entailed. I remember feeling like, this would be a sacred moment in his life which can't be messed up by flesh in any form. I felt like, when I carried his staff, I was carrying the ark of the covenant. It was sacred and holy. It was a moment in time God was honoring him and had chosen me to be a part of this momentous occasion. I was so honored to do it. I remember searching myself asking, "What do you feel, Chris? Do you feel anything other than happiness or joy for him?" I searched myself and it was true love that I had for him. It was not envy, nor jealousy, or even wishing it were me.

At the same time, it challenged me with God. It made me ask God, "What must I do to receive your favor for you to trust me again with your people? Would I ever pastor again? Would I ever have a moment with you that is sacred like this?" It wasn't a physical jealousy. It was a spiritual provoking pushing me to consecrate and seek Him more because I wanted a closer relationship. I didn't do it for personal gain. I wanted God to really be pleased with my life.

I remember my wanting to come out of my twelve-year sabbatical with God early and trying to literally push my way out, prematurely. I thought to myself, it's time for somebody to celebrate me because I've given my life to people. I felt like people owed me something and my family had suffered enough. I wanted a three-day birthday celebration. My wife and Bishop J. said, "Why would you want a birthday celebration for three days? You're not the Pastor." I became angry with them because neither one of them understood how I felt. When I tried to explain it to them, I used the scripture to fit my needs. I said, "Those that sow into your life spiritually shall reap your carnal." Not realizing that it was not my time to reap, I was still in the sowing season. I thought Bishop J, being my friend and my brother would have understood. What I didn't realize was that he was also my pastor and was hearing God for me in this season. God was telling him no, and I was telling him to do it.

Many times, I didn't understand what God was doing through him, so I questioned his methods and motives. From time to time, I was angry with him because I thought he should have done something differently. Unbeknownst to me, he was only doing what God permitted him to do. God humbled me to that place where he made me a sheep all over again. Where I was once shepherding a flock and a prophet of God, I had to come through that process of great humility. I humbled myself to the place where I became the servant more so than the one who was being served. I served him because I loved him. It was easy; it wasn't hard to sit and submit. It was an honor to serve him and carry his bags or iron his shirts. It wasn't hard to listen because he was full of wisdom that was beyond his years and I trusted him in this time of being vulnerable. It took me a while to realize that I was in safe place, and that God put me into the hands of someone who loved and supported my family and who would go beyond the call of duty for us.

God always chooses another you to humble you; a person who is just like you. Someone who is just as equal in strength, equal in power, and equal in authority. And that's exactly who Bishop J. was for me.

> God always chooses another you to humble you: a person who is just like you.

Proverbs 27:17 ESV

"Iron sharpens iron, and one man sharpens another."

Your Hour Has Not Come Yet

I remember arriving in New York City one cool Spring day. The weather was a little nippy from the after-effects of the lingering winter. I had been to New York City before, but this time it was different. I remember seeing so many different cultures of people. There were crowds of people everywhere. I'll never forget how the bright lights illuminated off the skyscrapers lighting up the entire night sky. When we finally arrived at the church, there were parking attendants that directed us where to go. In anticipation of our arrival, they already had a room set up for us. We were in the room until someone came to escort us out to our seats. As we sat down, praise and worship had begun. In the midst of praise and worship, I glanced at the pastor and saw that he was slouched over. Then, everyone ran to him to see what was going on. After a few minutes, they stretched the pastor out on the floor. The pastor had passed away right in front of the whole congregation. Immediately, everyone started praying and interceding. Bishop J turned to me and said, "He cannot die because you are here." I remember wanting to go up there to pray him back to life. As I was getting ready to move the spirit of the Lord spoke to me and said, "Be still, your hour has not come yet." I felt like I was being crushed into tiny little pieces because in my mind I thought I was ready. I was already four years into this sabbatical with God. I felt like it was about time for me to come out and for God to restore me back to where I needed to be. As I was standing there engulfed in my thoughts the people were praying for the reviving of the pastor, his pulse returned, and he was revived.

The reason why He told me my hour had not yet come was because He was working out character issues in my life Getting me ready for promotion. It was not time for me to be known as a healer, prophet or apostle of Jesus Christ. Your suffering is what validates you for promotion.

Remember, God never moves in your time. He only moves in His timing.

Bishop J was scheduled to preach the next day. As we were leaving to go to our hotel, Bishop J received a phone call informing him that he would be going LIVE on the Word Network. That night, he was given the opportunity to preach worldwide. He was so humble, all he wanted was a professional video of himself out of the deal. He didn't want the money or the popularity. I remember running out to help him prepare for that momentous evening. I was so happy for him; I felt like it was happening for me. While he was being recognized and respected, I stayed in the background, and although they knew me, no one ever addressed me. God didn't have them acknowledge me.

John 2:1-4 NIV

[1]On the third day a wedding took place at Cana in Galilee. Jesus' mother was there, [2]and Jesus and his disciples had also been invited to the wedding. [3]When the wine was gone, Jesus' mother said to him, "They have no more wine." [4]"Woman, why do you involve me?" Jesus replied. "My hour has not yet come."

My hour has not yet come:

Meaning not the hour of his sufferings and death, in which sense he sometimes uses this phrase; as if the hint was, that it was not proper for him to work miracles as yet, lest it should provoke his enemies to seek his life before his time; but rather the time of his public ministry and miracles, which were to go together, and the one to be a proof of the other; though it seems to have a particular regard to the following miracle, the time of doing that was not yet come; the proper juncture, when all fit circumstances meeting together, it would be both the more useful, and the more illustrious: or his meaning is, that his time of doing miracles in public was not yet; and therefore, though he was willing to do this miracle, yet he chose to do it in the most private manner; so that only a few, and not the principal persons at the feast should know it: wherefore the reproof was not so much on the account of the motion itself, as the unseasonableness of it; and so his mother took it.

Bible Study Tools

https://www.biblestudytools.com/commentaries/gills-exposition-of-the-bible/john-2-4.html

Aborting the Process

Now, it's about the ninth year into my sabbatical. At this time in my life, I felt like I had enough. Nobody could say anything to me about God. I didn't want to hear any prophecies. I didn't want anyone to give me a word of encouragement. I had completely shut down in my heart and in my spirit. All I could say is that I needed to provide for my family. So, I was going to make it happen my way. I was going to get a 9-to-5 job and work.

Therefore, I decided that it was time to leave Michigan. I had decided that we were moving back to Savannah to start the ministry again. I knew I had to come back to Savannah, but it was not the timing of God. I aborted the process. I held a revival thinking that the people were ready for me to come back. That service was jammed pack. As I continued having services, the attendance dwindled. I eventually moved the services back to the YMCA where we originally began our ministry. It was a sad state of affairs.

> It's not man that we seek, but His spirit for which we look for.

I remember I had my nephew stand outside waiting for people to show up, but the people were scarce. In that, God wanted me to know that it wasn't about the people. It's not man that we seek, but His spirit for which we look for. Was I going to trust people or was I going to trust Him?

As I was ministering, I thought it was my time, but God was still chastising me. I think we stayed about six or seven months at the YMCA, and I closed the church for the second time. Then, we moved to Atlanta. Although, God was telling me not to go from the very beginning, I left anyway and got a job. I was working at a Home Improvement establishment.

My aunt had told me that I could come up there to live with her and work to get my family a place to live. This is when God started dealing with me about integrity; being a man of my word. My aunt was teaching me about taking responsibility for my own actions. She made me live up to that standard. She said, "If the whole world was brought into existence on a spoken word, how much more powerful are your words that you speak out of your mouth. If you tell me something, mean what you say and say what you mean." God was taking me through a time of integrity and time management. My job required me to make sure I organized my time.

So, I had left from being a pastor of one of the fastest growing churches in Savannah to pushing buggies. I'll never forget, I had lost my car and had to catch the bus. I remember walking down those streets crying and asking, "Lord, where are You? Where am I? What's happening with me?" I saw some old members pass by me as I was standing at the bus stop. I imagined them thinking, *there was the Pastor that they once respected waiting to ride the bus.* That was hurtful. I remember being on the bus and being among the sheep, smelling like them, looking like them, tired like them, and lost like them waiting for a shepherd's voice. He had taken me out of the pulpit, and I felt as though I was a part of the sheepfold that had wandered away.

Every now and then, God would send me some water using people to give me an encouraging word. They would let me know that there was something special on my life and something different about me. It would be just enough to quench my aching soul and tired mind.

> Every now and then, God would send me some water using people to give me an encouraging word.

Chapter 4

The Preparation

One night, while asleep the Spirit of the Lord came into my room and said, "Wake up! I want to talk to you." That was the first time in twelve years that He spoke to me concerning me. I sat straight up. The presence of God was in the room and He said, "I want you to build me a platform."

I immediately said, "Oh my God, He's talking!" I jumped up quickly. I went to my nightstand and got a pad and pencil. I was shaking and crying, because this was the first time He had asked me to do something in twelve years! In twelve years! I started writing. I said, "I can do this! I can do that!" He said, "Wait a minute, hold up. Put your pen down. Put your pad down and listen to me." He asked, "What is a platform?" I said, "A center stage for one to be exalted and heard." He said, "That's what I want you to do for Me. I want you to start your healing crusade."

Right off the bat, He gave me a pastor's name to call. I called her on the phone and gave her my testimony about the last twelve years of my life. Right before I called her, she was in prayer and studying the Scriptures about being profitable for the Kingdom. She thought that word was for one of her ministers but as I told her how, seemingly, God had me on the backside of the mountains, invisible, voiceless, and tired. She knew it was for me and that God was saying I was now profitable for the Kingdom; that chapter in my life had ended.

2 Timothy 4:11 KJV

"Only Luke is with me. Take Mark and bring him with thee: for he is profitable to me for the ministry."

She was one of the most prominent pastors in Savannah, Georgia. She opened her entire church to me, paid for the entire crusade and gave me a platform to be able to do what God had called me to do. The services were packed and God did exactly what He said He was going to do. He healed, He delivered, and He saved.

Then God began talking to me about moving back to Savannah to pastor. God told me through a spiritual counselor, "This is the time." So, I came back and had a service with her and that's when God instructed her to put some of her honor on me.

Numbers 27:18-20

"And the LORD said unto Moses, Take thee Joshua the son of Nun, a man in whom is the spirit, and lay thine hand upon him; And set him before Eleazar the priest, and before all the congregation; and give him a charge in their sight. And thou shalt put some of thine honour upon him, that all the congregation of the children of Israel may be obedient."

That's when she informed me God said, "He was going to redeem the time, to give me time, to bring me back to time." We started having prayer and moving in the direction of ministry. There has been a continual flow and outpouring of His presence. We were in thirty-one days of fasting and praying and the Lord came to me again and said, "If they call you to Pastor, say yes." I woke my wife up and asked her, "What is God saying?" I didn't understand what He was saying. I was already a pastor; I was already doing what He asked me to do.

At this time, we were looking for a home and found this real estate company that happened to be connected to a church. I met the Apostle of that church and he asked me would I come in to be the pastor of their church. Immediately, I remembered what God told me and I said, "Yes!" The reason why He had me to go there is because this Apostle had revelation that was from the throne of God on the Church and Kingdom Age. He was able to give visions of the transformations and of the dispensations of the time in this hour. The visions God gave him were phenomenal. The revelation that he carried was second to none. He is amazing and full of God's presence. He's a worshipper that could bring in the presence of God.

God told him that it was going to take me two years to get the full understanding of the transition of the church coming out of the Church Age into the Kingdom Age. I had to come back into a place of submission. I cried like a baby because I couldn't believe God was asking me again to come submit to another leader; to stop being a pastor. It felt like I was being sat down again. I remember when I accepted, I had a congregation with whom I had to transition; I asked the Apostle if it were possible that I could come and sit down for a year. We were uniting two groups of people together and it was a definite cultural difference. I wanted them to understand that he was the leader…that he was the Apostle and I wasn't. As we merged together, it was necessary for us to build relationships. We were a family, coming together as one. I told

God, "I'm not moving anymore; I am here for life." *At some point you must stop moving and get grounded.*

In the midst of the transition, I had the date for my second crusade God was having me do already on the calendar. Meanwhile, I was given the responsibility of organizing and planning a crusade that my apostle was doing in Hinesville, Georgia. I was going to the meetings, setting up a venue, and making sure everything was in order for his crusade. I could not say anything to anyone about my crusade until God told me to reveal it. God told me not to worry about anything that I needed for the crusade. He said, "Take 100% of your time and put it towards the Apostle's project, to submit and commit to it, making sure that it lacks nothing." All I knew was to be faithful to his and God was going to bless mine.

Luke 16:12 AMP
"And if you have not been faithful in the use of that which belongs to another, who will give you that which is your own?"

While I was trying to get the contract signed for him, assuring things were in position for his healing crusade, I received a phone call concerning mine. The caller informed me to come and sign the paperwork, because my conference had been paid for in full!

The day of his crusade had arrived, and it was an outpour of God's presence. This is the time that I was grossly humiliated, though it was not intentional. During the illustrated sermon, a gray wig was placed on my head, and everybody started laughing. In this demonstration, I represented a religious Church that was old, gray and set in its ways that refused to change to the ways of God.

He had planned the entire illustrated sermon and thought that it would be funny. I could not get angry. I couldn't have an opinion about it. I couldn't even talk about it afterwards. I had to take it. The Lord admonished me to be and remain faithful.

When I walked into my crusade, the building was packed to capacity, with people everywhere. The power of God manifested in that place supernaturally. People were healed, delivered, and set free.

As time went on, so did the teaching and training. After the year had passed, the time came for me to step out and start pastoring the people. But the apostle told me, I wasn't ready because I have debt in my life, and I couldn't put that debt on the people. I had to sit down. I was crying like a baby saying, "Here it is, Anika. I'm being sat down by God again." I associated the pastor with the will of God. And I'm being sat down again after twelve years. "God, how did I fail you?" I felt so depleted and emotionally drained. It was the most miserable and heart-breaking feeling, but it was my apostle's teachings. I had to submit to it.

Immediately after receiving that word, I became diligent with my finances. I started fixing my debt and making sure I didn't have any outstanding bills. There was a lot of warfare that came from that. The persecution was fierce.

When I got cleared of my debts, he allowed me to attend the ordination class. I was already an ordained pastor and had to humble myself to be ordained under his apostleship. At first, I asked him was it necessary. He told me, yes, it was all necessary. I had to pass the class and his written test based on his teachings in order to be ordained. After passing the exam, my wife and I were ordained as pastors of the church. We were then allowed to have Sunday services. Through his teachings, I learned how to move the body of Christ from religion to a true, rich relationship with God.

My advice to anyone who is walking in this place of humility, walking into this place of honor… *honor those who are in authority. Honor those that have rule over you. Honor them so that God can honor you.*

All of this was what I had to go through to walk into this place *from humility to honor*. I had to come through my courses.

Second Benefit

That's when God gave me the vision for the ministry. The vision is, *"We are a ministry founded on biblical principles, Bible-based, Christ centered, and Holy Spirit led church. We are continually and consistently moving the body of Christ from religion into relationship, educating in kingdom revelation, leading the church with integrity and compassion in our community, our nation and our world."* That's when we officially started Resurrection Ministries of Christ Apostolic Center.

II Corinthians 1:14-15 KJV

"As also ye have acknowledged us in part, that we are your rejoicing, even as ye also are ours in the day of the Lord Jesus. And in this confidence, I was minded to come unto you before, that ye might have a second benefit;"

Since being at Resurrection Ministries again, I've seen growth, I've seen maturity, I've seen the presence of God, like never before. We moved into our new building and one of my spiritual sons brought a sign to the church that read

Resurrection Ministries of Christ Apostolic Center
Pastor Christopher Mike and
Elect Lady Anika Mike

As we went into the church, I looked at the sign and the Lord asked me a question, "Who is the Apostle?" I answered, "You are." He said, "No, I'm not. I'm above Apostles. Who is the Apostle?"

Immediately, I was reminded of something I heard, "Just because you don't answer God doesn't mean He doesn't expect an answer. That spirit will leave, and you must wait until He come around again to ask you. You don't know when that time is going to be." So, I didn't answer God. I just didn't answer Him. Because I didn't know what to say.

On another occasion, my spiritual counselor and I went to the bookstore and God presented the question again. I bought a Bible and for the engraving they asked, "What is your title?" At that time, I couldn't say. I knew He was calling me to the Apostleship, but I was not an Apostle yet. I knew that I wasn't a pastor because the passion had left me. I knew I

> Just because you don't answer God doesn't mean He doesn't expect an answer.

was operating as a prophet, but I didn't feel the weight of a prophet at that time. So, I said, "We'll just leave it blank."

One of my chief intercessors came to me and said, "It's time for you to step up; it's time to be the Apostle God has called you to be." I looked at her, but she had no idea what I was dealing with. She told me that God said, "It's time." That's how I came to this place of the affirmation service and coming into the place of being an Apostle.

PART II:

WALKING OUT THE PROCESS INTO THE APOSTOLIC

Chapter 5
The Way Up Is Down

Let us all be careful that we practice good leadership to the children as one with right authority under God. You cannot have authority unless you first submit to authority - therefore the way up is the way down.

Philippians 2:10-11

"...That at the name of Jesus every knee should bow, in heaven and on earth and under the earth, and every tongue acknowledge that Jesus Christ is Lord, to the glory of God the Father."

One of the hardest things to do is to submit to leadership who is full of personality. Although he is driven by the Holy Spirit, he may have his own way of doing things. For example, let's compare the earthly ministries of John the Baptist versus Jesus. John was the one whose voice cried out in the wilderness against sin. He would boisterously yell at the people, "Repent, you hypocrites, you vipers!" He prepared the way for Jesus who came with a different temperament.

Another example of this will be the charismatic lives of Dr. Martin Luther King Jr. versus Malcolm X. Both extraordinarily dynamic men were World-Renown activists who became the most vocal spokesmen and leaders in the civil rights movement. They both created platforms of recognition that resounded of equality, human dignity and physical sacrifice. Yet, they had different methodologies of getting their message to the masses. They fought against the same thing, the racist, deplorable ills of that day. One had a platform that heralded nonviolence, and the other's platform was compelled to answer the call to the front lines of the battle, by any means necessary.

I had to submit to several different types of leaders. They all had different personalities and temperaments. Although you may change leaders, you should always honor them with the highest regard and respect, because God once trusted them with the most precious thing, your soul.

This is why it is so important to have a spiritual covering. Many people have lost their confidence in Pastors and do not want to submit to God's order. He said, "I will give you Pastors after my own heart," and to "not forsake the Assembly of God." In this season, it has been a great falling away. People are leaving the church and staying at home listening to their favorite evangelist. Without having a pastor, people are going from church to church, eating from every table. This is detrimental to your soul and you'll find yourself in a very dangerous place. If you were to die this very moment, who will speak up for you? You will stand there with the accuser without anyone who will give an account for your soul. You think Jesus will be there? He will, but not as your Savior. He will be there only as your Judge.

Hebrews 13:17 NIV

"Have confidence in your leaders and submit to their authority, because they keep watch over you as those who must give an account."

A pastor must stand and speak on your behalf with the accuser of the brethren.

2 Corinthians 5:10

"For we must all appear before the judgment seat of Christ, so that each one may be recompensed for his deeds in the body, according to what he has done, whether good or bad."

Embracing the Shepherd's Rod

As we experience life, we find ourselves in many valleys, which can be discouraging. Sometimes, if we are not careful, it will lead us right out of the will of God. It takes discipline and corrections to stay in His will.

A shepherd's rod consists of a crook and staff and is used for the purpose of guiding the sheep. It gives the shepherd a longer reach to make sure the sheep are heading in the right direction. You must embrace this type of guidance because you have no idea what's ahead of you. Without the rod, you will go astray. The crook is used to catch the sheep and to bring them back into the sheepfold. Embrace the rod. It can save your life from the ravenous wolves that are waiting to devour you.

The shepherd also uses the rod as a form of correction. The word of God is like a crushing hammer. It was designed to beat us back into place. If you never accept  correction, nor allow yourself to hear how you have offended God, then God can never bring honor into your life. Chastisement never feels good at the time it is being administered. Your flesh never wants to be told what to do or feel pain. You must never pamper or bandage up your wounds. For growth, it is necessary to bleed, cry, and feel the pain. You must look towards God's Word to bring about change in your life or you will be stuck in your emotions and opinions.

Correction is not a rebuke all the time. It's just instructions to admonish you to do better. Remember, God chastens those whom He loves, according to *Hebrews 12:6.* Getting upset with leadership, or with someone who brings correction, is unacceptable. It is not them that you are rejecting. It is God. You must quickly resist your anger and embrace the moment of God's unconditional love.

God tells us to be submissive to *good and considerate* leaders, whether religious, political, or employment, as well as to those who are harsh. He asked a question, "For if we are only submissive to the *good and considerate*, what blessing is in it?" It's only when we are challenged that we make ground with God. It's like Him telling us to love our enemies and to pray for those that despitefully uses us, according to *Luke 6:28 KJV*. These acts are commendable before God. Because what we are doing is showing the world a better way and becoming a living sacrifice.

1 Peter 2:18–20 NIV
"Slaves in reverent fear of God submit yourselves to your masters, not only to those who are good and considerate, but also to those who are harsh. For it is commendable if someone bears up under the pain of unjust suffering because they are conscious

of God. But how is it to your credit if you receive a beating for doing wrong and endure it? But if you suffer for doing good and you endure it, this is commendable before God."

Whenever you find yourself under the leadership of someone who is forward or not so kind, it's because God is killing something in you. You must *"let patience have her perfect work, that ye may be perfect and entire, wanting nothing,"* as stated in *James 1:4.*

Never talk against leadership. God will always deal with His leaders. **James 3:1 says, *"Not many of you should become teachers, my fellow believers, because you know that we who teach will be judged more strictly."*** If you have been called to operate in the Fivefold Ministry, you have been given a work to do and your words carry a greater weight than those who are not of the Fivefold Ministry. *Ephesians 4:11* If you fall, you risk the chance of taking many people down with you. Therefore, God will judge you greater based on your level of influence and the kind of impact you had on those that you are inspired to lead.

You can't desire leadership for selfish motives nor personal gain. Those who used their positions as a source of manipulation and control already have received their reward on earth, fleshly gratification. *Matthew 6:2–4* Therefore, they will not receive anything in Heaven because they did not have the heart of God.

To be a leader, God takes you through the class of humility and brokenness, where you've

> You can't desire leadership for selfish motives or personal gain.

come to the point where you have nothing else to lose. You have relinquished and given up everything---your will, strength, and desires. You give God your all as a sacrifice.

Psalm 51:17

"My sacrifice, O God, is a broken spirit; a broken and contrite heart you, God, will not despise."

The Power of Spoken Words

According to the Huffington Post, "Words are singularly the most powerful force available to humanity. We can choose to use this force constructively with words of encouragement, or destructively using words of despair. Words have energy and power with the ability to help, to heal, to hinder, to hurt, to harm, to humiliate and to humble."

My Aunt Gee always used to tell me, "Chris, if the whole world was brought into existence based on the spoken word and if there is life and death in the power of the tongue, then your word should be just as powerful."

Proverbs 18:21

"The tongue has the power of life and death, and those who love it will eat its fruit."

If ever this scripture came alive to me, it was when I stopped to look at how damaged I was. I believed the lie, and if you are not careful you will too. Be careful of those pessimistic people who live and breathe to put you down. They never have anything positive to say. They don't celebrate your success; neither are they happy about your accomplishments. They are miserable and misery loves company. For years, I had allowed negative words and experiences to define me. I didn't realize that I was crushed, nor how it had affected me. I formed a negative opinion about myself. I lost confidence. It made me question my identity because of the name-calling and the ostracizing.

When I was in the fifth grade, I was challenged intellectually. My teacher told me I was dumb and tried to convince my best friend not to work with me on a school project because I was going to bring his grade down. It made me feel like I didn't have anything to offer. I was always the last one to be picked on a team playing any sports, and sometimes not even picked at all. I remember saying, "I feel like I was born without any gifts or talents." However, I am here to tell you, despite people speaking against you, being last and even being picked on, God has a purpose and a plan for your life. It was all in His will.

Jeremiah 29:11 KJV

"For I know the thoughts that I think toward you, saith the LORD, thoughts of peace, and not of evil, to give you an expected end."

> Understand this...
>
> anything broken can be fixed.

"When someone's spirit is broken, it is often done by physical, mental, emotional, sexual abuse - or by all of these methods. When a person's spirit is broken, they often feel they aren't deserving of joy, or they may have even totally lost all hope or desire for happiness; it's a feeling of total emotional defeat," as quoted by Williams Jenkins. Understand this...anything broken can be fixed.

Micah 4:6-8

"⁶In that day, saith the LORD, will I assemble her that halteth, and I will gather her that is driven out, and her that I have afflicted; ⁷And I will make her that halted a remnant, and her that was cast far off a strong nation: and the LORD shall reign over them in mount Zion from henceforth, even for ever. ⁸And thou, O tower of the flock, the strong hold of the daughter of Zion, unto thee shall it come, even the first dominion; the kingdom shall come to the daughter of Jerusalem."

The Lord was always near to my broken heart encouraging me. He kept His promises. So, when I hear the scripture say, "A healing tongue is a tree of life," I think of kind, soft words that encourage and build up. I think of motivational speakers that challenge you in a positive way. I think of God who enables, teaches and trains by His Spirit. Without Him intervening, I would still have negative thoughts and never would have walked into my true purpose.

Chapter 6
Seat of Honor

God works things in you that are well-pleasing to Him in your wilderness, for all things work together for your good, as admonished in *Romans 8:28.* You may not feel him, but He is closer than what you know.

When Paul says, "I learn how to be abased and abound," we only focus on being abased, but we never look at how we act in the abundance. Sometimes, having abundance can make one feel a sense of superiority. It can give you a false sense of pride.

In order to see yourself, the true you, **you must stop being the victim**. You must see your role in every situation. What did I do? What did I say? How could I have handled things differently? Pride will never let you see yourself, but it will always point out someone else's shortcomings. Why? Because your nose is always higher than theirs.

The Bible goes so far as to warn us that God hates the sin of pride

Pride will never let you see yourself.

and will discipline the proud! Let us not see ourselves as "wise in our own eyes," but let us become humble and willing to learn from God and others! That's what *Proverbs 3:7* states.

Pride is equivalent to someone starving for attention, respect, and someone who likes to be worshiped. Its very nature is to direct all attention to itself and make sure that its own desires are met. This selfish spirit will even move you to your own demise, simply because you were too stubborn to change your mind, your ways, and your spirit. When God is trying to kill the spirit of pride, He comes after everything that you have built for yourself. It could be your finances, looks, or your possessions.

Pride has been called the sin from which all others arise. Lust, envy, anger, greed, gluttony and sloth are all bad, the sages say. However, pride is the deadliest of them all. Pride is self-respect and self-esteem. Pride is also arrogance and hubris.

Proverbs 29:23 NIV

"Pride brings a person low, but the lowly in spirit gain honor."

How to Overcome Pride

How do we overcome pride? We must ask God to create in us a clean heart and to renew the right spirit within us.

Though pride is self-centered and stiff-necked, the only way to abolish this twisted perverted way of living is to find the virtue that pride protests against. A virtue that is lowly and not high minded, considerate and not stingy. A virtue that is loving and not spiteful. All these characteristics point to humility. With such a moral spirit that carries no malice, pride cannot possibly have entrance into your conscience to persuade you to become set in your ways.

By allowing the word of God to remove all selfish wills and desires, you must die daily. Every time you identify anything that exalts or promotes flesh or pride, you must deal with it immediately. Do not allow it to fester.

One of the hardest things to recognize and confront in ourselves is pride. For some of us, it has become a major part of our lives, sometimes without knowing.

Perhaps the most well-known warning is in Proverbs 16:18: "Pride goes before destruction and a haughty spirit before a fall"

Psalm 51:10, 17 KJV

"¹⁰Create in me a clean heart, O God; and renew a right spirit within me…¹⁷The sacrifices of God are a broken spirit: a broken and a contrite heart, O God, thou wilt not despise."

Many times, you don't know how messed up you really are. You must truly examine yourself. It's rather difficult to comprehend things when God begins to tell you what He dislikes about you. As God shines the spotlight of His Word on you, you must "mortify the deeds of the flesh." For example, the voice inside of you that says, "You're always right and everyone else is always wrong." If that's the case, then you're like God and nothing but pride is telling you that. Don't be puffed up with pride. But remember you are God's handy work. According to Psalms 51:5, "…*although you have been shaped in iniquity and conceived in sin*," you must be shaped and born again until you look like His image.

> ## You must be shaped and born again until you look like His image.

John 3:3

"Jesus answered and said unto him, Verily, verily, I say unto thee, except a man be born again, he cannot see the kingdom of God."

All in all, pride ought not to be our attitudes, but love is to be at the forefront of our minds to be humble. Submitting to those in authority, praying for those that despitefully use us, and killing every form of wrath with kindness.

How to Overcome Shame

Picture this! Jesus is sitting on the throne at the right hand of the Father, in Heaven. God looks at Him saying, "My people are in trouble, they need a savior." Jesus pondering within Himself, stands up and says, "I'll be the sacrifice." He humbles Himself to be born of a virgin, in a manger. Knowing from the very beginning, that he was doing this for a people who were going to put him up for public disgrace. This was a people who would not even receive Him or His sacrifice. *Wow, What a place of humility!*

Hebrews 12:2   ESV

"Looking to Jesus, the founder and perfecter of our faith, who for the joy that was set before him endured the cross, despising the shame, and is seated at the right hand of the throne of God."

He gives up His seat of authority to take the seat of shame. He suffered the shame and allowed himself to go through it because He knew there was another seat already prepared…A seat of honor! Understanding this fact, Jesus went through the shame, public disgrace, and the agony because He knew where He was headed. So, He endured the cross with the joy that was set before Him understanding the fulfillment of His assignment. Notice, His attention was not on His situations and circumstances. Therefore, your focus shouldn't be either. When you look to the left and the right, it causes you to be upset, confused, frustrated, and depressed.

Keep your eyes on the joy that is set before you and the promises of God concerning your life. Grasp the concept of not allowing shame, persecution, or disappointments to detour your focus. Continue to look towards the hills from which cometh your help, for all your help comes from the Lord. *Psalm 121:1-2* Then, you too can endure the shame of your cross.

What did Jesus do to shame? He despised it! The definition of despise is to intensely dislike, to regard with contempt. Despising shame is saying, "Shame, you are the fool! You have no voice or power in my life!" For Jesus, despising shame meant bearing the greatest symbol of social shame and disgust, the cross. When shame threatens to expose, humiliate, or devalue you, despise those false whispers. Have the courage and boldness to endure any shame, because in God's Kingdom, shame precedes glory!

> What did Jesus do to shame?
> He despised it.

II Corinthians 4:17 ESV

"For this light momentary affliction is preparing for us an eternal weight of glory beyond all comparison."

The only way that you will ever be able to handle this eternal weight of God's glory is being brought down low to be exalted. The process keeps you balanced, understanding that it was only God who delivered you. You must be willing to pay the price for what God is asking you to give.

I knew what I was asking Him for was going to cost me everything. And I said to Him, "Yes!" Because, if you can't handle the suffering, you will never be able to handle the glory. Know this, the glory is much heavier than the suffering.

> Know this, the glory is much heavier than the suffering.

Romans 8:18 KJV

"For I reckon that the sufferings of this present time are not worthy to be compared with the glory which shall be revealed in us."

The Bible says when you are buffeted for your own faults, take it patiently, as conveyed in **1 Peter 2:20**. It is only when you suffer for righteousness sake is when you will receive the reward of the Lord. You can always measure your anointing based on your humility and suffering for righteousness sake.

Chapter 7
From Humility to Honor

Proverbs 15:33 KJV

"The fear of the Lord is the instructions of wisdom and before honor is humility."

Part I:

What is Humility

The path of humility is the only way to promotion with God. You must be willing to make the ultimate sacrifice, giving up who you think you are and even who you think you should be. Many people think that God just passes out promotions like candy, but it doesn't work like that. He only gives promotion to those who are willing to pay the price, becoming nothing to become something. You must kill your own desires and will, for His.

Luke 14:11, NKJV

"For whoever exalts himself will be humbled, and he who humbles himself will be exalted."

How do you know that you are living in humility and ready to receive God's blessings?   Humility is the ability to be without pride or arrogance. It is a main character trait that should be seen in those who follow Jesus Christ. The best example of this is when Jesus humbled Himself and was baptized by John the Baptist. John the Baptist said, "It is not I that need to baptize you, but it's you that need to baptize me." Jesus bowed and kneeled and said, "Baptize me, John, so that the scriptures may be fulfilled." Here you see the King of Kings bowing to a human man. He humbled Himself to be baptized by flesh so that the Will of God may be done.

God takes you through the process of humility to prepare you for elevation. Always know that God is in control. It's not by your own strength. It is God who brings you out

> The path of humility is the only way to promotion with God.

and delivers you with His mighty hand. God knows exactly how much fire and molding it takes to make you His vessel.

Kathryn Kuhlman once said, "God is not looking for golden or silver vessels, but for yielded vessels. Yielded to the place where you will allow the Spirit of God to mold and shape you into God's creation and who He has called you to be in this earth."

Jeremiah 18:1-4 ERV

"This is the message that came to Jeremiah from the LORD: Jeremiah, go down to the potter's house. I will give you my message there. So, I went down to the potter's house and saw him working with clay at the wheel. He was making a pot from clay. But there was something wrong with the pot. So, the potter used that clay to make another pot. With his hands he shaped the pot the way he wanted it to be."

Humility will keep you in a place of repentance. The sting of your past will bring forth fear and keep you from stepping out to do what God has called you to do. The onslaught of memories of failure may cause a ripple effect to occur in your psyche, with your life falling like dominos with one fatal push.

Humility actually means that you feel confident in yourself. It's the act of being modest, reverential, and even politely submissive. Humility is the opposite of aggression, arrogance, pride, and vanity. Don't over-compensate. Serve expecting nothing in return; that leaves the power in your hands and out of others. In other words, if I don't expect anything from you, my feelings will not be hurt because I served and submitted to you.

Don't worry about being great or having a title in front of your name. It means nothing if you have no fruit. You must have the fruit before the title. The scripture says you will know them by

> The sting of your past will bring forth fear and keep you from stepping out to do what God has called you to do.

the fruit they bear, as quoted in *Matthew 7:16 KJV*. It's what helps you to identify your calling and who you are to God. The call will find you; you don't have to chase the call. Your life is already speaking of who you are because you're passionate about certain things. Your passion, the thing that moves you and what you enjoy doing, helps define your identification. If you pay attention to your passion, you already know what you are called to do because God moves in your passion. You pray and ask God to lead and direct you in your purpose.

Humility opens you up to hear and to understand the heart of God in every situation. Only those who are the beloved of God are called to do a great work for the Lord. Something you say, something you do causes you to reach the heart of God. It comes through great humility and great suffering. You must know how to get into that secret place, in God's heart. That comes through relationship and humility. Humility is the key that unlocks God's heart because pride certainly doesn't. "He who dwells in the secret place of the most High shall abide under the shadow of the Almighty." *Psalms 91:1* You will not be able to enter the secret place with pride. "For He resists the proud and gives grace to the humble." *1 Peter 5:5*

Humility is considered a heart thing. As a result of that, it causes you to have complete control over your attitude, prospective and actions. You have nothing to prove, but everything to offer.

1 Peter 5:6 (NLV)

"So, humble yourselves under the mighty power of God, and at the right time he will lift you up in honor."

I had to go through God's courses and classes of being humble, loving my enemies and praying for those who despitefully used me, according to *Matthew 5:44 KJV*. God will use people that will challenge you. I had to be brought down to a low place in order to be elevated. These classes are necessary, and you can't skip grades with God.

Humility is not a weakness, but it's strength in control. It's not allowing yourself to be taken to a place where you feel like someone is using you or even taking advantage of you. When you are walking in humility, you are walking in freedom from the desire to impress others and having to always be right. Many people will mistake this as a weakness, that you are naïve and don't have an opinion or a voice. Their arrogance and pride make them feel superior. But what they don't know is, you are in control and you hold the power of wisdom. You have enough wisdom and power to control yourself and your emotions.

Proverbs 11:12

"When pride comes, then comes disgrace, but with the humble is wisdom."

I have suffered enough to know how to be in control, that I don't offend God or make the same mistakes again and must repeat a course from which I had already been delivered. Everything that I went through was necessary for me to be able to handle what God is putting on my life today.

Jesus carried His humiliation in our stead. The bible depicts the horrific details of His dreadful trial, His conviction by Pontius Pilate before the people who once loved Him, and His ultimate death by crucifixion on that fateful day on Golgotha's Hill. He carried our sin to that rugged cross, bearing the fretful shame, disgust and humiliation for us that we may be reconciled back to The Father. He had to carry the very thing He would die on and that's what we must be willing and obedient to do.

Part II:

What is Honor

You asked the question, "What is Honor?" When you have honor, you don't have to be the winner or the one exalted. You respect others and their titles. In God's house, there are not only vessels of gold and silver but also of wood and clay. And some for honor and some for dishonor.

II Timothy 2:20, 21 KJV

"But in a great house there are not only vessels of gold and of silver, but also of wood and of earth; and some to honour, and some to dishonour. If a man therefore purge himself from these, he shall be a vessel of honor sanctified and fit for the masters use and prepared to do every good work that God has called you to do."

In your wilderness, you may not feel Him, but He is closer than what you know. To have honor is to give God honor. To honor God is to respect His Word and to trust and to esteem Him above all others. Above Him, there is no God. God is faithful and He would not let you be tempted beyond your ability. He will always provide a way of escape that you may be able to endure it. Even Jesus said, "My God, my God why have you forsaken me."

I Timothy 6:12 tells us to *Fight the good fight of faith*. That means that you stand firmly on the Word in Spirit and in Power. Come through the course. Get rid of your feelings. Get rid of your own reasoning and your own ideas concerning the issue. Therefore, you must have a certain amount of joy in order to pass your test. Without that joy, you can't even enter the classroom to take the exam. You must have joy.

Paul said, "I learned to be content in whatever the circumstances," in ***Philippians 4:11***. I didn't let it go to my ego or my pride. I learned to give God the glory. You must give Him all the glory and all the honor. You honor Him through taking care of the poor.

Proverbs 14:31

"He who oppresses the poor taunts his Maker, but he who is gracious to the needy honors Him."

Giving to the poor is another biblically explicit way that you honor God. It is important to note that this responsibility is ascribed to the Church and to individuals. You also honor the Lord through giving.

Malachi 3:10b NASB

"test Me now in this, says the LORD of hosts, if I will not open for you the windows of heaven and pour out for you a blessing until it overflows."

We are to honor God in a way that is proportionate to what He gives us, of time, resources, and with our life. Your tithes have the power to rebuke the devourer in your life. Your offering is the thing that brings in your increase. Then, the Bible said that your increase, for honoring God, will be press down, shaken together and running over. God is honored by your material gifts in support of His purposes to take the Gospel throughout the world. God is honored by your taking care of the less fortunate; and speaking His glory from your lips. These are ways we ascribe to Him dignity; this is how we honor God. You exalt others above yourself and that makes you truly worthy for promotion.

Chapter 8
The Office of An Apostle

What is an Apostle? The word Apostle means "the sent one." An Apostle is a special messenger and representative of the Kingdom of God. He is to establish and build churches. Not buildings, but people, because the people are the church. He births out churches on the foundation of biblical principles. He operates in miracles, signs, and wonders with deep revelatory experiences from God. He is humble and a servant of the Lord, Jesus Christ.

According to Kenneth Hagin's book, "*He Gave Gifts Unto Men,*" the three qualifications and signs of a true Apostle are: one must have signs, wonders, and mighty deeds, one must have very deep experiences with The Lord, and one must have seen The Resurrection.

I believe, it started out with the Apostles and it's going to end with the Apostles. In the Latter-Day Saints movement, an Apostle is a special witness of the name of the Lord Jesus Christ and one who is sent to teach the principles of Salvation to others. In the Latter-Day Saints church, an Apostle is a priesthood office of high authority in the priesthood hierarchy.

For me, to be a servant of God is to serve with compassion and with love. The days of celebrity Apostles, Prophets, Evangelists, Pastors and Teachers are over. God is no longer going to allow it. I'm glad I'm living in this day and time to be an Apostle when the season is changing. It's a celebrity mindset wanting an entire entourage of people around you with no message, no power and no presence. I want those around me who can raise the dead, heal the sick, and cast out demons, right along with me. That's the help I need in the spirit. Those are the armor bearers God wants in this hour.

I'll never forget, I was asked to serve this evangelist as she was getting out of the car wearing a mink coat with a cell phone in her hand. Her armor bearer was behind her struggling to carry her bags. That's when God told me, "You will never be like this." He asked me, "What is wrong with her hands and why can't she help this young girl carry her bags?" He then said to me, "I will resist the proud and deny them access to the ultimate power of miracles, signs, and wonders." The gifts of God are without repentance. One of the greatest deceptions, is believing that you are operating in the power and anointing of God. On the contrary, you are operating in the spirit of divination, not recognizing you have been denied God's presence. In all actuality, the gift is not for you. It's for God's people. For example, when Jesus was walking and the woman with the issue of blood touched Him. He felt the virtue go out of Him and asked, "Who touched Me?" If that woman can touch Jesus' garment, who are we that we can't be touched?

I believe that we are living in the time now where God is allowing His power to manifest again in the same manner but even to a greater measure of His Spirit. We must reach a desensitize generation that has no reverence, fear or honor for God.

Isaiah 48:11 NIV
For my own sake, for my own sake, I do this. How can I let myself be defamed? I will not yield my glory to another.

The Scripture tells us that He will do this for His namesake. I remember dreaming that an angel came and got me. He told me to hurry up because I was late. As this angel pushed me into this room, they began to wash me. It was the purest water I had ever seen. The water was so light you couldn't even feel it. Then they robed me and took me into another room. This room was full of elders and priest presenting me with a gift that was wrapped in white linen. When I opened it up, it was the most beautiful set of keys that I'd ever seen. And then a voice came from out of nowhere and said, "for these are the keys to the kingdom respect and cherish them always." Then I awakened.

Jesus spoke to the Apostles in ***Matthew 16:19 KJV "And I will give unto thee the keys of the kingdom of heaven: and whatsoever thou shalt bind on earth shall be bound in heaven: and whatsoever thou shalt loose on earth shall be loosed in heaven."***
This scripture is often misinterpreted that a believer can bind or loose things in Heaven and on Earth. We must remember Jesus spoke those words to the Apostles. Like in a natural home, keys are only given to those that can be trusted. Apostles had been given the keys to God's Kingdom because they could be trusted. Only God's true Apostles have the ability to bind and lose.

We can see its unique purpose in their ministry demonstrated in places like Acts 5, when Peter confronts a deceptive believer. In Acts 5:1-5 Peter "binds" a believer to a judgment of physical death for his deceptive practices in the church.

I believe that this is the authority that has been given to the Apostles. To those who can be trusted with such power. They carry a mantle of humility and have paid the ultimate price, their life.

A lot of people desire the office of an Apostle because it is one of the highest positions in the church. People don't realize that to truly walk in this office one must be tested and tried by the Lord. Yes, that may sound easy, but He sends enough fire and persecution your way to burn out any desire for fame, fortune, or glamour. When He's finished with you, you just want more of

Him. You know that without Him, you can't do anything and that the power He has invested in you is for His edification. So, when the weight of your office sets in and you are in high demand, the power has fallen in the house, lives are being changed, limbs begin to grow, blinded eyes are opening, you quickly humble yourself and give God all the glory.

The Apostle has a one-on-one relationship with God. They converse and God gives them instructions. Then, the Apostle carries them through. I have found that it is very important for Apostles to have an advisory board, a Presbyterian counsel. You must not be short of this, because the power and authority can go to your ego. The counsel is needed so that you can bounce the how's, why's, and when's around to make sure you stay on the straight course with God. This counsel must be a group of people whom you trust and that also has a level of God on their lives. You may ask, "Why do I need a counsel if I'm hearing from God?" I'm glad you asked. You must be accountable to someone so that you don't go off on your own tangent, with your own revelation based on the situations in your life. The counsel is also there to help you process the revelations given to you by God.

Proverbs 11:14 KJV

"Where no counsel is, the people fall: but in the multitude of counselors there is safety."

As one of God's leaders, you must be able to see those that God has placed around you because they have a voice and can hear God, as well. It's the same gift that works within all; iron sharpens iron so that one person sharpens another, according to the scripture in **Proverbs 27:17**.

Romans 1:1 NIV

"Paul, a servant of Christ Jesus, called to be an apostle and set apart for the gospel of God..."

Now that I have been called to the office of an Apostle, it demands a level of consecration. I've been ministering for thirty plus years to others and now that ministry is turning around and saving me too. Should I preach this word and myself be a castaway? God forbid! Now, I must fast more and spend more time with God. It also mandates that I walk in a place of purity and truth. I've started shedding off people and all distractions that will make me live beneath the privilege of the honor and respect of which God is calling me. I'm being pulled away from friends, family, and church members into a place in God where He's demanding that I go into my prayer chambers and shut the door behind me with no one else, just Him and I.

My job as an Apostle is to see you fulfill your destinies and watch you get in position for God to use you in the greatest measure possible. I will be able to see, train, push, support financially and in love without a motive to help you get in position of who God is calling you to be. It will also be my job to really see you reach that place in God. Can you imagine the power of us working in ministry together to see God's vision come to past?

I see the vision clearer now. I know who I am, and I make no apologies for it. Once in five a.m. prayer, a very powerful prophetess said to me, "Pastor Mike, the devil is going to be scared of you when you find out who you are in God. It is very easy to lose yourself and self-worth when you don't know who you are and who's you are. You must know without a shadow of a doubt that you have a purpose."

I Corinthians 9:1-2 MSG

"And don't tell me that I have no authority to write like this. I'm perfectly free to do this—isn't that obvious? Haven't I been given a job to do? Wasn't I commissioned to this work in a face-to-face meeting with Jesus, our Master? Aren't you yourselves proof of the good work that I've done for the Master? Even if no one else admits the authority of my commission, you can't deny it. Why, my work with you is living proof of my authority!"

The Final Words

Personal Messages from the Writing Team:

Joyce, C.
Odom, E.
Okwu, A.
Pritchard, J.
Wynn, D.

Joyce, C.

What I felt while assisting in the process of writing *"Humility to Honor"*, was that of many feelings. God, you really allowed me to assist with such an intimate part of your man servant's life! God I'm grateful! I'm grateful for you allowing me such an opportunity to be a part of something much more than myself. Being an assistant of such a humble yet powerful Man of God who is full of love, is an honor and I'm thankful for it. Each day as we met and worked on *"Humility to Honor,"* I became more and more humble. I saw myself in many of the chapters. I saw where God was showing me how pride is well versed, and it is something that can very well be hidden inside. I constantly became more and more thirsty for the knowledge that God imparted through *"Humility to Honor."* Many other things I learned as Apostle Mike was very transparent in his process. I learned honor isn't something that is just given, but it is earned and God judges this. The path of humility is sometimes portrayed as the low path, but it is the path God uses to bring forth his divine will and purpose for our life. This read will not only put weapons in the hands of the servants of God but will teach the servants of God how to use the weapons given. This book will also give lessons on how to succeed in the spirit and in life according to the word of God. In areas where I felt I was humble, I was not. I was indeed a first part-taker of God's release and impartation through *"Humility to Honor."* Apostle Mike, thank you for allowing me an opportunity to take part in this, an ordained book from God himself. This reading is based on real life experiences and Rhema Revelation from the Holy Spirit.

My prayer is that many lives will be touched and changed forever to the glory of God, the Father of Heaven and Earth.

God's Blessing.

Cheers, here's to completion!

To countless hours we all spent in the office brainstorming, typing, proofreading and hearing you say to me, "Eden, wake Up-ah!"

The joy that lit up within when we clapped to celebrate progression as you poured out your heart to complete each chapter.

To the uncontrollable group laughter from the stories you told.

The random singing.

Eating my favorite trail mix for energy.

My experience was invaluable. Thank you for your vulnerability. Sharing your personal moments and every impartation we received that lifted off the pages into our hearts, minds and spirits.

Congratulations Apostle Mike!

Okwu, A.

To Apostle Christopher Mike:

I am so honored and privileged to have been able to have the great opportunity that so many others have not. To be able to see up close the transformation that God and only God has done. I have seen the transformation performed through the creativeness of God through people (whether of His spirit and direct lessons and interventions, prophesies and experiences) or through the works of Satan and his evil devices and schemes. I've seen prophecies fulfilled and spoken ones that are yet to come! I've seen people come and people go; Promises made and promises broken. I've seen you laboring in the field and I've seen you at home in the church. All the while He has prepared you for such a time as this.

For years you have said, "Amethyst, we got to write this book, we've got to start writing my book!" That time never was the right time, until now which is the God Appointed right time.

I now see why the book never came together at those times. It is because the story had not been written and the life and experiences had not been lived. As I sat and listened to you tell your story of life, of transition, of true transformation, consecration, from pride to humbleness: Just to look, to listen and then to become truly broken by your words, your life, your experiences. It brought forth true deliverance in my life too. You know that each time that you entered into the room to work, the presence of the Lord would meet us all. I will never forget the time spent with you and the rest of the writing team bringing this long-awaited vision to past. I know that this book will minister, deliver, give hope and clarity to all of those that open to read.

It is with the utmost honor that I call you my spiritual father, my friend, my pastor, my Apostle! Again, thank you for allowing me to be a part of such a life-changing moment in God's time. May God continue to bless you as He elevates you to the next level in Him.

Pritchard, J.

What a privilege and an honor It has been to work along-side and contribute in creating this literature with my Apostle, Pastor Christopher Mike. The content of this book is so inspirational and heart-felt, that it is impossible to not walk away changed with a new way of thinking. I pray that everyone who comes in contact with this book will have allowed the Spirit of God to teach and embrace you in the ways of humility. Just as Jesus walked on this earth. May the grace of God be with you and I want to thank and pray a special blessing to Apostle Christopher Mike.

Wynn, D.

It has been a great honor and a privilege to have been able to assist
Apostle Christopher Mike in completing his first book. Helping
him has helped me. I thank God that I was able to be one of the
first partakers of this memoir. It's truly a manifestation of God's
glory. The richness, and the in-depthness and the transparency in
this book is uncanny. Just from sitting and listening to the different
experiences and encounters he had with God has impacted my life
Tremendously. Some of the things that I thought I knew about
myself is not who I am.

Reading this book has caused me to re-focus my attention on who I
am and on who God has called me to be. It caused me to look at
my life and upbringing in a more humbling perspective; actually
deal with certain issues that I had swept under the rug and hidden
in my heart.

Through this opportunity I was able to gleam and learn from his
testimonies. Through the similarities, I was able to find myself.
Many times, as he was speaking, we could feel the very presence
of God in the room. We would get stuck at a portion of the book
because it became just that real. As we were having the writing
sessions, we applied his stories and wisdom to our lives. The
wisdom and the knowledge that he has, and he shared in this book,
is irreplaceable. I'm forever changed, and I hope that by you
reading this book you have been impacted and changed, as well.
So, because Pastor Mike overcame, so can we. God brought him
through, He'll bring us through, too.

Although I may not say much, I'm soaking it all in. The long, late nights were so worth it and I'd do it again if given the opportunity. And I dare not take it for granted. But in all sincerity and gratefulness of the heart... Thank you, Apostle Mike and I applaud you on a job well done!!!

Closing Remarks to Writing Team

Pastor Christopher Mike

To my faithful book committee
This would not be possible had you all not been faithful. The countless hours that you all sacrificed, staying up late, eating trail mix, between Eden reading in her newscasting voice and Demetrius being very patient with us when we got off the subject, because Clinton and Jacob wouldn't stop joking around. Thank you, Anika and Amethyst, for always having my back and pushing me to finally complete my first book.

Appendix

Introduction:

1.) PRIDE. Pride is the spirit that caused Satan to be cast out of heaven and the very same spirit that has compelled many today to be resisted by God. Satan fell because of pride that originated from his desire to be God instead of a servant of God. www.all.aboutGod.com>history-of-satan Copyright 2002-2019

Chapter 1:

1.) Mainstay: a person or thing on which something else is based or depends.

Collins, H. (Ed.). (2019, 10 08). *Dictionary.com*. Retrieved 10 08, 2019, from www.Dictionary.com: www.dictionary.com/browse/mainstay

2.) Pitty Pat is the national card game of Belize. It is played by from two to four players with a standard 52 card pack. Though it may not be apparent at first sight, Pitty Pat is essentially a rummy game with a similar mechanism to conquian, in which the objective is to make three pairs starting from a five card hand.

www.pagent.com/rummy/pitty pat.html

@John McLeod , 2003. Last updated : 9th August 2003

3.) General Missionary Baptist Convention of Georgia, Inc. Headquarters: 155 Joseph E. Lowery Blvd NW Atlanta, Georgia 30314
(404) 524-5571
Post Office Box 92340 Atlanta, Georgia 30314
(404)688-4212
email: headquarters@gmbcofgeorgia.com
website:gbcofgeorgia.org

Chapter 2

1.) General Missioary Convention of Georgia Men's Retreat
Land of Promise
3411 City of Refuge Road
Culloden, Georgia 31016
(478) 885-2555

2.) Definition of *apostle*
   1: *one sent* on a mission: such as

a: one of an authoritative New Testament group **_sent out_** to preach the gospel and made up especially of Christ's 12 original disciples and Paul

Merriam-Webster Dictionary
Copywrite 2019 Merrim--Webster, Incorporated
www.merriam-webster.com/dictionary/apostle

3.) Resurrection Ministries of Christ, Inc
First Established: December 7, 1996
May Street YMCA
1110 May Street
Savannah, Georgia 31415

Chapter 3:

1.) Adjutant: The root of adjutant, is Latin juvare "to help, support." Role of an adjutant to the pastor also known as the armorbearer; serves his pastor or leader in any way possible; he acts as a spiritual equivalent to a personal assistant most commonly serving in the protestant church.

December 31, 2018
Careertrend.com

2.) Aborted the process: To abort something is to end it. When something is aborted, it's finished. When you abort a plan or activity, you're ending it, usually prematurely.

Vocabulary.com
https://www.vocabulary.com/dictionary/abort
© Vocabulary.com

3.) Humility: freedom from pride or arrogance : the quality or state of being humble; *Humility* means "the state of being humble." Both it and *humble* have their origin in the Latin word *humilis*, meaning "low."

October 7, 2019
Merriam-webster.com

Chapter 4

1.) Sabbatical: that sabbatical is related to Sabbath, which refers to the Biblical day of rest, or the seventh day. We trace the origins of both sabbatical and Sabbath to the Greek word sabbaton. Sabbaton itself traces to the Hebrew word shabbāth, meaning "rest."

October 7, 2019
Merriam-webster.com

A spiritual sabbatical is about removing the busyness of life and standing still in the Lord. A spiritual sabbatical will help us grow closer to the Lord so that we can better hear His voice and follow the right paths He has for us. When we are on this sabbatical, we are journaling our experience and expectations for growth. We don't intend to remain the same as we were before the spiritual sabbatical. This time will bring balance back to our lives so that we can be ready for the next season of God's grace.

Daughters of the Creator
https://daughtersofthecreator.com/a-spiritual-sabbatical/
Copyright ©2015 Telling Ministries LLC.

Chapter 5

1.) Shepherd's staff

123RF
https://www.123rf.com/stockphoto/shepherd_staff.html?sti=mzw93ay7rpzghml37g|
© 123RF Limited 2005-2019.

2.)

Dr. Martin Luther King Jr.

An American Christian minister and activist who became the most visible spokesperson and leader in the civil rights movement from 1955 until his assassination in 1968. He played a key role in the American civil rights movement from the mid-1950s until his assassination in 1968. King sought equality and human rights for African Americans, the economically disadvantaged and all victims of injustice through peaceful protest.

Born: January 15, 1929 in Atlanta, Georgia
Assassinated: April 4, 1968 in Memphis, Tennessee

App.pureflix.com

History
https://www.history.com/topics/black-history/martin-luther-king-jr
November 9, 2009

3.)

Malcolm X

An activist and outspoken public voice of the Black Muslim faith, challenged the mainstream civil-rights movement and the nonviolent pursuit of integration championed by Martin Luther King, Jr. He urged followers to defend themselves against white aggression "by any means necessary."

Born: May 19, 1925 in Omaha, Nebraska
Assassinated: February 21, 1965 in New York

History
https://www.history.com/topics/black-history/malcolm-x
October 29, 2009

Chapter 8

1.)

Kenneth Hagin

He Gave Gifts Unto Men

Pages 16 & 35

<u>3 Qualifications and Signs of a true Apostle:</u>

1. One must have signs, wonders, and mighty deeds

2. One must have very deep experiences with the Lord

3. One must have seen The Resurrection

2.) Armor bearers: Church pastors or ministry leaders select armor bearers to support them, especially with prayer. They are so named because in Old Testament times, kings selected certain officers to stand with them in war and to bear their armor. An armor bearer needs to be sensitive to this and know his leader, even before he accepts the job of an armor bearer. Many armor bearers travel with their leaders to assist them with all aspects of service and ministry. A long-term commitment will benefit both the leader and the armor bearer.

(Lisa)Thompson, Elizabeth. "What Is the Job Description of an Adjutant to the Pastor?" *careertrend.com*, https://careertrend.com/about-6718448-job-description-adjutant-pastor-.html. 8 October 2019.

Scripture Reference

Scriptures used in this book:
All scriptures are quoted based upon the King James Version bible unless duly stated or notated

Chapter 1:
Job 33:15-17

Chapter 2:
Jeremiah 1:5
I Corinthians 1:27

Chapter 3:
Galatians 5:22-23
Luke 16:12 AMP
Proverbs 27:17 ESV
John 2:1-4 NIV

Chapter 4:
2 Timothy 4:11
Numbers 27:18-20
Loke 16:12 AMP
2 Corinthians 1:14-15

Chapter 5:

Philippians 2:10-11
Hebrews 12:6
1 Peter 2:18-20 NIV
James 1:4
James 3:1
Ephesians 4:11
Matthew 6:2-4
Psalm 51:17
Proverbs 18:21
Jeremiah 29:11
Micah 4:6-8
John 2:1-4 NIV

Chapter 6:

Romans 8:28
Proverbs 3:7
Proverbs 29:23 NIV
Psalm 51:10,17
Psalm 51:5
John 3:3
Hebrews 12:2 ESV
Psalm 121:1-2
2 Corinthians 4:17 ESV
Romans 8:18
2 Peter 2:20

Chapter 7:

Proverbs 15:33
Luke 14:11 NKJV
Jeremiah 18:1-4 ERV
Matthew 7:16
1 Peter 5:6 NLV
Matthew 5:44
Proverbs 11:12
2 Timothy 2:20,21
1 Timothy 6:12
Philippians 4:11
Proverbs 14:31
Malachi 3:10b

Chapter 8:

Proverbs 11:14
Proverbs 27:17
Romans 1:1
1 Corinthians 9:1-2 MSG

Resurrection Ministries of Christ Apostolic Center Inc. Re-established: December 24, 2017

Our Vision

We are a ministry founded on biblical principles, that is Bible based, Christ centered, and Holy Spirit led. Committed to moving the body of Christ from religion to relationship, educating through Kingdom revelation, and leading the church with integrity and compassion for our community, our nation, and our world.

Mission Statement

To equip the body of Christ to mature independent living, naturally, and spiritually

Our Statement of Faith

We believe the Bible to be the inspired, the only infallible, authoritative Word of God. We believe that there is one God, eternally existent in three persons: Father, Son, and the Holy Spirit.

John 11:25

I am the resurrection, and the life: he that believeth in me, though he were dead, yet shall he live

What is Pride?

Biblical Definition: An inordinate self-esteem; an unreasonable feeling of superiority as to one's talents, beauty, wealth, rank, and so forth; disdainful behavior or treatment; insolence or arrogance of demeanor; haughty bearing. Pride can, more rarely, have the good connotation of a sense of delight or elation arising from some act or possession.

Synonyms of pride: egotism, arrogance, haughtiness.

Teacher), J. O. (2018, October 8). *What is the Biblical Definition of Pride.* **Retrieved from Quora.com: www.quora.com**

Pride

noun

\ 'prīd \

Definition of *pride*: the quality or state of being proud: such as
a: inordinate self-esteem : CONCEIT
b: a reasonable or justifiable self-respect
c: delight or elation arising from some act, possession, or relationship parental *pride*

2: proud or disdainful behavior or treatment : DISDAIN

3a: ostentatious display
b: highest pitch : PRIME

4: a source of pride: the best in a group or class

5: a company of lions

6: a showy or impressive group *pride* of dancers

WORKS CITED

Collins, H. (Ed.). (2019, 10 08). *Dictionary.com.*
    Retrieved 10 08, 2019, from
    www.Dictionary.com:
    www.dictionary.com/browse/mainstay

Incorporated, M. W. (2019, October 8). Retrieved
    from www.merriam-
    webster.com/dictionary/pride

https://thecelebration.wordpress.com/2010/01/08/w

    hats-in-your-attic/

Johnson, N. (2019, January 1). *Moving From the
    Church Age to the Kingdom Age!* (The
    Academy of Light) Retrieved October 8,
    2019, from
    HisKingdomProphecy.com/moving-from-
    the-church-age-to-the-kingdom-age/:
    www.HisKingdomProphecy.com

Motyer, S. (1996).
    biblestudytools.com/dictionary/call-calling/.
    (W. A. Elwell, Editor, & BakerBooks a
    division of Baker Book House Company)
    Retrieved 10 10, 2019, from
    biblestudytools.com:
    www.biblestudytools.com

Teacher), J. O. (2018, October 8). *What is the Biblical Definition of Pride*. Retrieved from Quora.com: www.quora.com

What is the Church Age? (2002-2019). (Got Questions Ministries) Retrieved October 13, 2019, from www.Gotquestions.org: www.gotquestions.org/church-age.html

Wikipededia, the Free Enciclodedia. (2019, 10 08). Retrieved from wikipedia.com: en.wikipedia,org/wik/Batman

Wikipedia, the Free Encyclepodia . (2019, September 16). Retrieved from Wikipedia: en.wikipedia.org/wiki/superman

Wikipedia.com. (2019, September 16). Retrieved from Wikipedia, the Free Encycopedia: en.wikipedia.org/w/index.php?title=Publicat ion-history-of-wonder-women &action=history

Made in the USA
Columbia, SC
25 February 2022

56835617R00074